Wendy Geller, Dorothyjean Cratty, Jared Knowles

Education Data Done Right

Creative Commons License

Education Data Done Right: Lessons from the Trenches of Applied Data Science

This book is for all the hardworking data folks who show up every day and do what it takes to leverage administrative data well in service to public education.

Contents

List of Tables   xi

List of Figures   xiii

Preface   xv

1 Welcome   1

   1.1 Introducing Education Data Done Right 2

   1.2 So, who are we and why did we write this book? 3

   1.3 Why you should keep reading this book. 6

   1.4 What's in this first volume, anyway? 8

   1.5 What we hope you'll take away from this book. . 9

2 The Holy Grail of Data Science: Rock Solid Metadata and Business Rules   11

   2.1 Introduction 11

   2.2 Metadata and You (this is a forever relationship) 13

   2.3 The Living Data Dictionary: Syllabus to Your Work 16

      2.3.1 What Does a Good One Look Like? 16

   2.4 Data Management 19

      2.4.1 Sound Analysis: Grinding for the Good of the Metadata 23

      2.4.2 Provide Continuity 25

2.4.3   How You Can Do It   26

2.4.4   Tools to Consider   28

2.5   Documented Business Rules: The Data Scientist's
       Handbook   30

2.6   Conclusions   32

2.7   Appendix   33

3   An Analyst's Guide to IT   35

3.1   Introduction   35

3.2   Groundwork   36

3.3   IT 101: Speaking the Same Language   40

3.3.1   Business Rules   40

3.3.2   Change Management   42

3.3.3   Database   43

3.3.4   Data Governance   45

3.3.5   Data Integrity   47

3.3.6   Data Warehouse and/or Operational Data
         Store   48

3.3.7   Enterprise   49

3.3.8   ETL   49

3.3.9   Version Control   50

3.4   IT 102: Strategies for Successful Collaboration with
       IT   51

3.4.1   Bring IT in From the Beginning   53

3.4.2   Play Up the Cool Factor   54

3.4.3   Get Creative with Resources   55

3.4.4   Use Their Processes and Procedures to Get
         it Right   57

3.4.5 Build Informal and Formal Channels of Communication 58

3.5 Conclusion - What to Take Away From This Chapter 58

4 Data Requests: You Can Make Them Useful (we swear) 61

4.1 Introduction 61

4.2 Taking a different perspective 62

4.3 Prioritizing and Triaging Requests: Data Governance to the Rescue 65

4.4 Check Before You Wreck: Why Levels of Granularity Matter 68

4.5 How to Respond to the Request 71

4.6 Managing Data Requests 72

4.6.1 Publish Data 72

4.6.2 Collect Requests in a Single Place 73

4.6.3 Inventory Common Requests 74

4.6.4 Automate Common Requests 74

4.6.5 Use Request Approval to Build Data Governance Decisions 75

4.7 Use the Data Sharing Agreement for Good . . . 75

4.8 Closing Thoughts 80

5 Politics and Data Driven Decision Making 81

5.1 Introduction 81

5.2 What Do We Mean By "Politics"? 83

5.3 Politics 101 86

5.3.1 Policy Windows 86

5.3.2 Credit Claiming and Failure Blaming . . . 87

5.3.3 Loss Aversion and Incrementalism 88

      5.3.4   The Role of Information   89

  5.4 Key Practices   92

      5.4.1   Humility   93

      5.4.2   Repeated Engagement   94

      5.4.3   Coalition Building   95

      5.4.4   Reputation Management   96

      5.4.5   Timing   97

  5.5 Conclusion   98

6 Moments of Truth: The Importance of Descriptive Statistics   99

  6.1 Introduction   99

  6.2 Why write this chapter? 101

      6.2.1   Because the data's origin story matters. . 101

      6.2.2   Because modeling is better with fewer guesses 106

  6.3 The power of descriptives: Nobody puts crosstabs in a corner 108

  6.4 Describing your data early and often 110

  6.5 Three handy rules for leveraging descriptives . . 116

  6.6 Words can't describe... 121

7 Applying Tools of the Trade: Descriptive Data Commands in Context   125

  7.1 Introduction 125

  7.2 Describing your data – what this looks like in practice 126

      7.2.1   Two types of descriptives 126

      7.2.2   Keeping it real (in the abstract data sense): 130

7.2.3   Command-relevant shorthand for data elements 134

7.2.4   Descriptive tools 137

7.2.5   Descriptions: summary statistics 138

7.2.6   Depictions: graphs of distributions and relationships 143

7.3   Conclusion 147

8   Conclusion   **149**

8.1   Metadata 149

8.2   Analyst's Guide to IT 150

8.3   Data Requests 151

8.4   Bureaucracy and Politics 152

List of Tables

2.1   A data dictionary you can start today   34

7.1   Categories of descriptive tools and data compo-
      nents   126

7.2   Numeric variable types   135

7.3   String variable types   135

List of Tables

List of Figures

4.1 Internal and External Stakeholders   63

5.1 The Organizational Perspective on Cost and Benefits   91

6.1 State legacy system of linked administrative records by grade and year. 103

6.2 Graph confirms what assumptions about high school test records miss. 105

6.3 Commonly used test files needed course records to match teachers. 113

6.4 Analytic output should be transparent about sample cohort attrition. 115

6.5 THE graph. 122

7.1 Simple histogram shows class size increasing with smoothed gifted-program ratio. 129

7.2 Simple stacked bar graph shows student programs throughout class sizes. 145

Preface

Acknowledgements & Reviewer Bios

Acknowledgements

This book couldn't have happened without the generous time, expertise, and good humor of some truly talented folks. While many of them are among our respective families (who put up with our bi-weekly calls eating into the dinner hour [pun intended] and read many, many drafts), others are thoughtful colleagues that unabashedly told us when our ideas needed a whole bunch of work and when they weren't half bad too.

So to our families, thank you Alex, thank you Sonya, and thank you Hannah. You're the best spouses a bunch of nerds could ever wish for. We mean it.

We send our gratitude to those we love, who supported us, who tore the work apart, helped us improve it, and who raised a glass with us when we'd had too much "screen time". We are better because of you.

To our respected colleagues in data, who reviewed and provided their incisive feedback, who don't pull any punches and can smell a lazy line of code a mile away, thank you for your brilliance, your commitment to excellence, and for holding us accountable.

To our copyeditor, Lindsey Mae Brownson, thank you for your laughter, your patience with us as we tried to explain why or how our silly metaphors and analogies worked, and for joining us on this first foray into saying something we hope folks will find useful.

Thanks for throwing your oar in with ours and giving a damn about people reading.

Reviewer Bios

We couldn't have completed this book without help from the following expert reviewers who tested our ideas and gave us the feedback we needed.

G. Matthew Snodgrass[1]

With a Master's in Statistics and a PhD in Public Policy and Management from Carnegie Mellon, G. Matthew Snodgrass is an analytic strategy consultant focused on driving value through economic and statistical modeling in the natural resource and energy sectors. Beyond pure quantitative analysis, he engages in risk assessment, risk management, and the development of negotiation positions for his clients. This guy knows his math and how to use it! Yowzah!

Andrew Laing[2]

Blazing the trail as the very first Chief Data Officer for the State of Vermont, Andrew got his start in Engineering. Today, he enables the State of Vermont to realize the value of its rich data assets through enterprise information management, data governance, and operational intelligence. His specialties include systems thinking, business systems architecture, modeling, and engineering, GRC, MDM, DevOps, portfolio management, and being one of the kindest, most patient people you'll probably ever meet.

Melissa Straw[3]

Melissa Straw is the Director of Data Warehouse and Decision Support at Wisconsin's Department of Public Instruction. With over seventeen years of experience managing and leading large-scale data warehouse and business intelligence projects, Melissa is an expert at delivering data products that improve decision making.

---

[1] https://www.linkedin.com/in/g-matthew-snodgrass-a6776778/

[2] https://www.linkedin.com/in/andrewnathanlaing/

[3] https://www.linkedin.com/in/melissa-straw-kijewski-98789a/

She has spent the last seven years overseeing a team in charge of building and expanding the statewide WISEdash Data Dashboard and Data Warehouse solution. Schools and districts use WISEdash for improvement planning, early warning identification, in addition to snapshot and data quality reporting. The team is also tasked with meeting federal and state reporting requirements, as well as maintaining the public-facing dashboard. In addition, Melissa has focused expertise in implementing proven organizational data governance and data quality solutions.

Lindsey Brownson

Lindsey is a recent graduate of the Vermont College of Fine Arts MFA in Writing and Publishing program, where she practiced across genres but concentrated in creative non-fiction. Her final thesis project was a 108-page memoir in essays titled Why Are You So Emo. She was a fiction reader and a member of the copyediting staff for the 2018 edition of Hunger Mountain, VCFA's annual literary journal. She also had the opportunity to intern at The Wendy Sherman Agency in NYC as a reader for in-process fiction manuscripts being prepared for publication. She considers it a privilege to have other writers hand their hard work to her with implicit trust, and couldn't have been more excited to help with this project.

Nick Maskell[4]

Nick is a graphic artist with an associates degree in graphic design, and a bachelors in fine arts. For the last four years he has worked as a full time designer/illustrator at Susi Art, a custom apparel company in Massachusetts. Since graduation, he has worked across multiple platforms on a wide variety of projects ranging from corporate marketing and ad campaigns, to coloring books and birthday invitations. Working with our authors, he designed the EDDR logo and the cover for this book, as well as some of the visual elements within it. If you would like to see more of his work,

---

[4] https://www.nickmaskell.com

or are in need of a freelance designer, please visit nickmaskell.com[5] for more details.

And thank you to Daniel Jarrat for detailed correction of typos that appeared in the first version of this text as well as incorrect placement of footnotes.

Author Bios

Wendy I. Geller

As Director of the Data Management & Analysis Division, I serve alongside my Work Family of Data Scientists as a centralized resource to the Vermont Agency of Education. My crew collects, stewards, and leverages the institution's critical data assets to create and share data products that enable empirically-based practice and policy decision-making.

We lead, partner with external bodies, and execute on the analytic activities of the institution as well as plan, develop, and manage the data governance program and the business side of the DataOps continuum.

My Ph.D. (2011) is in sociology from the National University of Ireland Maynooth (www.nuim.ie) where I was a doctoral fellow at the National Institute for Regional and Spatial Analysis (www.nuim.ie/nirsa). My dissertation findings highlighted shifting demographics in education arenas and labor markets internationally, specific education orientations occurring across cultures, and presented thoughts on the social and spatial forces surrounding rural community viability.

Since leaving academia, I've dedicated myself to creating the cultural, infrastructural, and operational conditions needed to care

---

[5] https://www.nickmaskell.com

for and use data sustainably so as to provide value-added analyses in the public sector.

My specialties include DataOps generally, data governance, data privacy, applied research, program evaluation, social policy, management, and developing functional relationships with IT/kind-of-being-part-of-IT-but-not-really.

Dorothyjean (DJ) Cratty

Through the nascent DJC Applied Research LLC[6] and in partnership with other firms, I conduct research in education, labor, and public economics for and with local and national agencies and organizations, helping them and their stakeholders develop relevant actionable findings. As part of this work, I advise states and districts and their university research partners and grantmaking organizations on collaborative data analytic methods for their researcher practitioner partnerships (RPPs) tailored to their specific data sources and needs.

Currently, I lead the education data audit and analysis stage of the District of Columbia's aspiring research collaborative, with Data Ethics LLC. In similar prior work, at AIR, I led the development of Rhode Island's cross-sector Research Hub. At Duke University, I built out North Carolina's cross-sector research capacity as the data and methods specialist on an interdisciplinary research team with the statewide data center. As a program officer for the federal Statewide Longitudinal Data Systems (SLDS) grant program, I worked with state agency data and research managers to help develop and share best practices for collaborative cross-sector research.

My Smith College undergraduate economics thesis studied ten years of state employment and work injury records to assess effects of workers compensation benefit reductions on claims relative to injuries. I completed the PhD economics coursework at the University of Maryland, and left without a dissertation to work

---

[6] https://www.DJCAppliedResearch.com

as a staff economist for the research division of the World Bank. My country studies there included determining the cause of sudden high dropout rates among extremely poor households and estimating labor productivity costs for war-torn populations. Journal publications include the Economics of Education Review and Economics of Transition.

The focus of much of my research has been on equity of opportunity and resources, with studies specifically designed to answer actionable questions that practitioners, policymakers, and stakeholders ask of the data. These questions of varied access and returns require more nuanced data derivations than are often carried out sufficiently in academic research studies. My direct service to clients is helping them use the empirical facts of their fully prepped and vetted data to qualify existing claims and generate more grounded findings. Some of these detailed data methods and findings papers available on the SSRN open source site[7] are found to be useful resources by other state and district data analysts.

Jared E. Knowles

I currently serve as the founder and president of Civilytics Consulting LLC[8], the data science consulting firm I founded in 2016. Civilytics serves clients at all levels of government in policy areas such as K-12 education, higher education, policing, and taxation. Before founding Civilytics, I worked for 6 years at the Wisconsin Department of Public Instruction. There, I pioneered an award-winning machine learning algorithm that is used across the state to help struggling students get back on track. Since 2012, this work has been used around the country to improve the accuracy of predictive analytics systems in education.

My work has been published in several peer-reviewed journals, including the Journal of Educational Data Mining and Journal of Policy Analysis and Management. I received a Ph.D. in Political Science from the University of Wisconsin-Madison in 2015. My

---

[7] https://papers.ssrn.com/sol3/cf_dev/AbsByAuth.cfm?per_id=1589079

[8] https://www.civilytics.com

dissertation investigated the untapped democratic potential of school board elections and the conditions under which school governance in the United States becomes democratic.

Now, through Civilytics, my work focuses on building the capacity of public sector partners to sustain analytic products after the initial work. By using open source software and open data sources, providing all source code and extensive documentation, and excellent training of customers in the product, Civilytics ensures that its clients can maintain products developed long after the contract ends. This sustainable partnership model is unique, allowing agencies to build lasting organizational change. Civilytics approaches projects with a human centered design methodology that creates lasting partnerships with clients.

CHAPTER 1

Welcome

You. Yes, you there. Isn't it exciting? You are sitting down at your desk at your new job as an education data analyst. You've been trained in so many statistical methods, you're a wizard with R or Stata, you can adjust standard errors with the best of them — you've got this. Plus, now that you are working at an education agency, you don't have to sift through a tedious IRB and data request process — you can get started right away doing powerful analyses that will improve the decision making of your institution.

As you turn on the computer and drink your coffee, you are filled with anticipation. You've already requested all of the longitudinal assessment data from IT so you can get a jump start. You open your email, eager to download the data and get started, but instead you see:

"About that request for data — we'll need you to be part of a data governance discussion with us. The attached data includes a number of shifting definitions and cannot be used for year to year comparisons at this time."

Data what? Definitions? The field names are all the same, so what's the problem here? You take a deep breath and Google "Education data governance" and now, you're here.

Welcome.

We've all been there.

Let's talk about what comes next.

1.1   Introducing Education Data Done Right

The profession of education data analysis is growing rapidly. In our opinion, it is richly rewarding and also highly challenging. Every day, in cubicles across the country, with bad coffee and no ball pits to play in, data analysts are busy helping education leaders make better decisions. This is noble work, but in our experience, a gap exists between what many think this work means and what it actually is.

There's the idea of running Bayesian multinomial probit regression models with millions of records of data seamlessly reported out in beautiful illuminating dashboards for all to see, and then there's the reality — carefully documenting changes in the data collection process, reconciling student enrollment counts across collections, arguing with outside researchers about what the data can and cannot say, and answering public data requests instead of doing what you had mapped out for your week.

This can be a hard difference to realize, and our own wrestling with it was part of why we decided to write this book.

Don't get us wrong — we're fans of hierarchical classification models to inform education decisions, but there are plenty of books to help you with that part of the job.

We wrote this one to help you do the "work before the work" so that when you fit that model, you know the underlying data are solid and the results are actionable, because frankly, there is an awful lot of work to do before you can start that kind of analysis. And, now that you're in this role, people will actually trust and take actions from the results.

We learned that lesson the hard way (well, at least some of us did) and we're here to help you find processes you can use to streamline those efforts, so you can spend more time answering challenging questions and less time sleuthing through ancient

PDF documentation of old data collections. Or worse, have no documentation to go by at all.[1]

1.2   So, who are we and why did we write this book?

Well, in short, we are probably a lot like you. We are all academically trained social scientists who studied hard and then transitioned to working in education agencies — you can get our full bios here.

We met up years ago at the annual STATS-DC conference hosted by NCES one day where we found each other through our shared griping about some of the blind spots we saw in how data were being used for decision-making in K-12 education.

From a shared moment of recognition in a too-cold DC hotel conference room to a dinner and drinks conversation afterwards, we realized we'd found our Tribe and we decided we needed to do something. Truth be told, that moment crystallized around Jared and DJ expounding upon how they were trying to help connect state and district data analysts to share work. They recounted many of these people coming up to them after presentations about analytic work they had done with the data, to discuss how they too had done really well thought out analysis, documented it thoroughly, and used it to provide stakeholders with insights regarding the strengths and limitations and suggested next steps.

After many, many hours of pouring their hearts and souls into these projects, for many of them the end result was the stakeholders going in the direction they had initially considered before the thoughtful analyses (which was to say, in the opposite direction). And in many cases even local policymakers were more swayed by national high-profile research findings based on only the slightest grasp of the complex local data that were used to derive the

---

[1] https://en.wikipedia.org/wiki/Alien_(film)

findings. It was the same situation playing out in different states with different stakeholders! Powerful analysis derived very intentionally from a deep understanding of the local data was not the driving resource for improvement it seemed it could be. What in the world could be going wrong, we all wondered? It was at that time Wendy, the newest of the crew, piped up and said "Wow. That's like trying to give a wrench to a horse."

After much laughter and deep commiseration, we figured we should try to do something about what we felt was an unfortunate situation. We decided to form an organization to help develop "tools of trade" so to speak, and a better understanding of the need for these important approaches and practices. There are lots of associations and conferences and the like for academic data analysts, but not something comparable for those of us in the applied realm. So we created DATA-COPE (Data Analysis Technical Assistance Community of Practice in Education) — catchy right? It became a gathering place for others like us — analysts working in this field who saw the disconnect between their academic training and the needs of their organization.

We also started to use the wrench analogy when talking about our work because we thought it helped folks realize that succeeding in this field is about rolling up your sleeves, doing the hard work, and tightening up the "bolts" of our organizations' respective infrastructure. Ours is like the role of the engineer in turning architectural theory and real materials into useful things that don't fall down. This is also why we made sure it had a place in this book!

Over the years, at subsequent conferences and via phone calls in-between, we realized that our experience was indeed shared across the country (read: it wasn't just our little group!), and that there were many more talented, thoughtful, smart analysts working in isolation in LEAs (Local Education Agencies) and SEAs (State Education Agencies) all throughout the nation. It became clear through our conversations on our online user-group forum that there was great demand for a resource that was specific, incisive, and might help us all cope a little better with the daily grind we find ourselves in. We decided that someone needed to make that resource we all kept talking about. So, we turned our energies from updating the DATA-COPE site toward focusing on writing this volume. We decided it was possible to do (or at least we would try really hard at it, calculating a minimum tear investment of 3.8 liters at most). And now we're here, sharing our collective experience and hard-earned chagrin!

It wouldn't be honest of us if we ignored the fact that a big motivation for writing the book was our collective frustration with so much of the commentary that is out there about education data analysis. We've read research reports that ignored key data definitions, excluded records by mistake or without justification, or derived a variable by adding together two misinterpretations of other variables — all with data we had spent years of our professional lives shaping, analyzing, and understanding.

It troubled us that big policy decisions were being made based on regression results built with shaky analytical samples. This happened not out of any malicious intent, but out of a lack of understanding — an understanding that we knew was quietly shared by our (mostly unsung) peers across the country.

So, we decided it was time to get loud about it and encourage folks everywhere to do better science. That's the thing about education data analysts working in public service — we're mostly a quiet bunch (people who know Wendy will laugh at this sentence).

We don't give each other prizes and awards (no Early to Mid-Career Distinguished Analysis of Attendance Data Award yet, though Jared's always thinking about ways to boost the recognition of this kind of work).

We don't call up news outlets to ask them to report on the savings we've made for taxpayers by increasing the precision of enrollment counts.

Many of us aren't allowed to even attend conferences or meetings with our peers to exchange ideas — settling instead for the occasional webinar while we eat a reheated lunch at our desk because the budget just won't stretch to support the flight, hotel, and per diem rates to cover the trip.

But, if we don't speak up, our voices will be lost among those who do and we think that would be a shame. This book is our contribution to the myriad discussions out there going on about what it means to be able to make "data-based" or "data-driven decisions."

We're taking our experience and putting it out there for everyone to see; take it or pass it by as you see fit.

It's an opinionated tour through our hard fought battles and lessons learned as we each worked in environments shifting from a focus on data collection and reporting to meet basic compliance, to one of trying to leverage data to inform decision making. We've focused on the roads less traveled in this first volume — how organizations think, how you can shape them, and the role data, metadata, and data governance play in policy and practice. We've got lots of thoughts on growth models, early warning systems, dashboarding, and reporting tools, but our first premise is that if you don't start with doing the basics well and consistently, well "garbage in, garbage out" is a tired cliche in most of our work at this point, right?

1.3   Why you should keep reading this book.

As you might have gathered from the opening few sections, this book is different.

First, it's a living document — this is the 2019 edition. Each year, we plan to work with experts in the field (maybe you?) to add chapters and update the book for the new year. The field is changing rapidly, and we need a publishing approach that fits with those changes.

Something more substantial and crafted than a blog, but less stodgy and slow than a book in an academic press. So, we're using LeanPub — you pay what you want for the book, and you get free updates as we add new content. If you want a printed version of the book you can order a print-on-demand copy as well.

This approach has two big advantages. First, you can be part of this book. See a typo? Let us know and we'll fix it and give you an acknowledgement. Have a resource to share that would fit well in one of the chapters? Send it in and if we include it, we'll credit you.

We can update the book as frequently as we like between full releases or new editions — fixing typos, adding resources, and improving it as we go and as a community of practice.

The real value of this approach comes when we hear from you. We are offering this book as a gathering point for conversation, as a way to spark interest, share knowledge, and as a means to find more people like us and get their great ideas heard so they can help others.

So, in short, we invite you to please contribute.

A second advantage of our approach is that you can use this book however works best for you.

We believe in creating a resource that works for our colleagues across the country (besides, everyone knows there is no money in writing books these days).

What's important to us is not the extra cup of coffee we might be able to buy someday (maybe) from the proceeds, but how the book can be used by you to help you in your important work. Take the book, give copies to everyone on your team, hold discussion sessions with it, print it out, and share it if you find it useful.

Use it however you like. All we ask is that you don't redistribute it commercially and that if you use it and like it, please make sure to give us some attributions as authors and maybe drop us a note letting us know how you used it. That's it!

1.4   What's in this first volume, anyway?

This first volume attends to topics we feel aren't covered well enough in other volumes, blogs, resources, and materials we've found and reviewed. We also think that these topics are critical to success as an education data analyst and, honestly, as an analyst in the applied environment in general really. They're the stuff we've heard our friends and colleagues from all over the country struggle with and represent our experience with addressing questions that you can't really "Google" or take an online course to learn about (both excellent resources by the way and which we use regularly).

Each chapter has been reviewed by at least one expert whom we have asked to check our work — see the reviewer biographies to learn about the bad-ass people whose expertise helped make this book better in every way.

So where are we kicking this conversation off? Our first chapter is like a dive into the frozen lakes of Vermont or Wisconsin (where two of us are from, so we know) — metadata. Metadata is a critical, core component of a data governance strategy, and probably the best place to start any data governance project.

The next chapter covers IT operations and is followed by our address of the dreaded data request — often framed as a tedious chore, but if you channel your inner Judo master, it is actually one of the best ways to enact some important organizational change on a lowkey basis.

Then we tackle "the bureaucracy" and all of its glory — decisions about data are political decisions. If you recognize this and use some of the approaches we suggest, we think they'll help make your job as an analyst easier!

Finally, we close with two chapters that discuss some of the methodological pitfalls that inspired us to put fingers to keyboard in the first place and advise on handy tips you can use in your job tomorrow (or today, or whenever you're back in the office).

We'll take you on a tour of some of the key techniques needed to do quality descriptive analyses that don't discard inconvenient data, but deal with it head on. This serves as a nice transition between the work you need to do to contextualize your data, and the work you want to do next with it — analyses that lead to actionable insights.

This book is not an academic study of how education data professionals do their work — it's the missing manual we each wish we had when stepping into this work. So you won't find citations of studies in education journals. You won't find a methodology section. You'll find our collective experience carefully crafted through hours of revisions and hours and hours of conversations with our peers and mentors.

One of Us

In support of the ideas we put forth here you'll find "One of Us" sections scattered throughout the book — a specific anecdote from one of the three authors illustrating the point being made.

These sections are marked off with special formatting. Jared's really proud of that part.

1.5   What we hope you'll take away from this book.

Ultimately, we hope you finish reading this text and have a feeling that you're not alone, you're not crazy, and that you're equipped with enough information to start engaging in the kind of data management and governance that will enable you to do analytic work that won't fold up in a stiff breeze.

Academia might have prepared you for a lot of things, but this environment is different and it can be disheartening and unsettling to find that out. We hope you read this and keep the faith.

We hope you take away encouragement and community from this book.

We hope you'll be inspired to (keep) do(ing) sound science in service to the public sector because we care about all those of us who harness our powers for the forces of the greater good and we value your success.

We value it because each of our individual successes is a success for all of us when we share it. We value it because we believe that we are better together.

We hope that you take away and consider our invitation to join this conversation, and our opening offer is some advice on a few of the less spoken about topics that we hope you find useful immediately in your day-to-day.

We hope you see colleagues and collaborators in us, as public-service minded social scientists who felt like so much of what it takes to do good applied analytics wasn't discussed enough and who wanted to talk and share about that foundational work.

We hope you feel like you've found a network of analysts and you'll be excited about contributing to our story together. Each chapter is a beginning, to open up thoughts and connect you to new ideas or resources to help you on your path. We hope you'll consider sharing what has worked for you in the aspiration that it works for someone else out there too.

We hope this work will help you in finding creative ways around seemingly impossible tradeoffs. We hope it supports you in rigorously evaluating education programs that seem to spring up to suit every need. And, most of all, we hope you'll find what we've shared useful and that it helps you do good work.

The Holy Grail of Data Science: Rock Solid Metadata and Business Rules

2.1 Introduction

Some may scoff at this chapter. This is unwise because there are good reasons we titled it "The Holy Grail of Data Science".

To start, the Grail[1] is a mythical thing that is supposed to provide everlasting goodness or life (depending on what you read) and or represent some kind of lofty objective or goal far greater than anything directly benefiting oneself. To these ends, comprehensive and well-stewarded metadata and exhaustive business rule documentation are much like the Grail. They are elusive — it's not terribly likely that any institution is going to have these in reality — but institutions and good analysts should aspire towards them in the everyday, because they serve a purpose much more durable and important than any of our individual tenures as an employee ever will.

Furthermore, just as most lore usually follows the heroics of some special and talented characters, this kind of existential work requires the combined knowledge and talent of the key people who care for the institution's data if it's to be done successfully. Once you find and bring together the combined wisdom and skills of the folks who have been tending to the organization's data, something truly special can happen.

At first blush, many won't think this chapter sounds all that much

---

[1]https://en.wikipedia.org/wiki/Holy_Grail

like the stuff of legends. Yet in our experience, the diligence and fellowship you cultivate around the work we discuss here will be the foundation of something extraordinary for data use in the applied environment.

This is because the work you and the other stewards or analysts can do together to discover, capture, and codify these critical pillars of the institution's information assets won't just help you do better work, they will empower others around you for years to come.

You are more powerful together than you are in isolation. With this work, what you build as a united group will help others create their own analyses in sound ways as well as reduce the overhead required to connect the data to new and diverse other sets. Ultimately, it will enable investigation of questions you haven't yet asked (or didn't have the time to explore).

So, to help you get started on the journey this chapter invites you to take, we'll discuss the basics of what we think about metadata (there are a surprisingly abundant number of ways[2] you could define it), why we believe it's important, and what you can do to help steward it well. We'll also talk about how we understand business rules (which also have surprisingly abundant definitions), why they're a critical part of how you work with metadata, and how they should inform any analysis you plan to do. Knowing them will help protect you (and your readers) from performing poorly constructed analyses and they'll shield you from hours of wasted work because they help you see beyond the numbers.

To that end, in the following sections we'll also try to help you set realistic expectations for the maturity level of this kind of work and documentation in any given institution. We'll also note that this work is never "done"; there are only so many hours in a day and the realities of limited resources can be stark. Those challenges don't mean we shouldn't strive to leave things a little better than how we found them though, and the following sections provide some suggestions about how you can contribute to doing just that

---

[2]https://en.wikipedia.org/wiki/Metadata

for the analysts that will come after you. In the next sections we'll lay out why we think it's worth answering this call to adventure[3] with a resounding "yes".

2.2 Metadata and You (this is a forever relationship)

At their heart, metadata are kind of like the Force[4]. They are the stuff that binds your work, penetrates it, defines it, and holds it together so it can blend with other work to create something greater than itself alone. So, perhaps they are actually more of a force multiplier[5], if you will. They help everyone do their part of the work better, together.

When documented and shared effectively, they save a TON of time, especially when you have to repeat analyses year over year. They also help you limit down time when you have turnover in staff or need to move work around your team. In fact, one way you can begin building your fellowship of stewards is to share your documentation together, learn from one another, and begin building the corpus of what it takes to carry out your organization's work on an annual basis. This way, your people do not remain your processes and you become able to help one another in a way you may not have been able to otherwise.

While so far the reasons for doing this work might not be as lofty as considering the inherent value of metadata, let's be honest, turnover is hard for teams and organizations, time is valuable, and the less you have to spend on figuring out what actually happened the last time a workflow was carried out, the better you're positioned to be able to tackle value-added work in the

---

[3] https://en.wikipedia.org/wiki/Hero%27s_journey

[4] https://en.wikipedia.org/wiki/The_Force_(Star_Wars)

[5] https://en.wikipedia.org/wiki/Force_multiplication

long run. Here is one place you can see immediate return on investment.

All that being said, setting realistic expectations about what and how your colleagues think about and relate to metadata will be important if you don't want to be disappointed by the varying interest and depths of knowledge that different folks might have on the subject.

For example, if you ask just about anyone who works with data, "what are metadata?" you'll probably get the stock response of "well, they're data about data". But "data about data" can mean A LOT of things to A LOT of different people who work with data throughout its lifecycle. To a developer colleague of yours in IT, metadata could have to do with types, lengths, comma delimited values, pain in the neck special characters, the validation processes, and relationships that the data will have to other objects in a data model.

To a database administrator (DBA) they could be anything from privacy requirements due to data sensitivity — to backup schedules, storage requirements, and primary and surrogate keys[6].

To an analyst, they might be codeset values or information you'd expect to find in a data dictionary, information about whether the data were self-reported or collected in another fashion, and whether there is missingness in the set (which there can sometimes be, and let's be honest, it's rarely random, so MICE procedures[7] can only go so far to help.).

The point is, for having such a snappy, colloquial definition as "data about data," metadata can be a very complicated topic and you'll want to be conscious of who your audience is and what their work encompasses when you talk to them about it. It's also the kind of knowledge that can make or break your analytic plans as we discussed in a later chapter on building good relationships with IT.

This is because what the data are, how they can and can't be used,

---

[6] https://en.wikipedia.org/wiki/Surrogate_key
[7] https://www.ncbi.nlm.nih.gov/pmc/articles/PMC3074241/

and what their strengths and limitations might be are all critical data about those data.

But beyond being thoughtful about your relationship with your IT data colleagues, not knowing the data well enough before you begin your analysis can mean you're setting yourself up for failure or worse, that you could be drawing false conclusions from the data set. This is why it's critical to review what documentation exists about the data you're hoping to use before you set to work. Leverage what the folks who came before you have left for you, even if it's sparse and incomplete.

We encourage this especially because if you don't know the data well enough, you could be asking too much of them or asking them the wrong things entirely and using them in a way they were never designed to support. This is a serious pitfall. Don't try to scratch your back with a lightsaber[8].

To help you be as empowered as possible in using data well, what we'll offer in this chapter are some basics that we learned (sometimes the hard way) are critical to get right. If you do the basics well, then your analysis has a strong foundation to build upon. This certainly won't be an exhaustive discussion, but we'll share what we've found to be some of the most essential elements to setting yourself up for success in the long term.

The first thing we'll note is the powerful role a robust — and living — data dictionary can and should play for any data team. The second is a high-level overview of what business rules are and why you should not just know about them, but document and maintain them carefully. Lastly, we'll reflect on how solid metadata and business rule documentation are critical parts of the data governance[9] infrastructure that can help take an institution from a condition where data and their management are ad hoc, to one where the institution is poised to leverage them for innovation[10].

---

[8] https://en.wikipedia.org/wiki/Lightsaber

[9] https://en.wikipedia.org/wiki/Data_governance

[10] https://drjdbij2merew.cloudfront.net/PCIO/PCIO_Mag_Fall2016.pdf

2.3   The Living Data Dictionary: Syllabus to Your Work

2.3.1   What Does a Good One Look Like?

Like we introduced at the beginning of this chapter, what we're about to recommend achieving and stewarding here, in our experience, is as elusive as the Grail.

But we're going to say it anyway, because it's important to have ideals so you have something to aim for, right?

Every institution should have a living and well-cared for data dictionary; a good one is like a thoughtful syllabus. Without a detailed and clear syllabus, how would you know what to expect of a course? How are you supposed to know what it is about, how it is structured, which modules depend on others (make sure you understand those), when your due dates for work are, and how in the world you are supposed to know what it is going to teach you?

Without it, you won't know any of these things and what you'll have to end up doing is to muddle your way through often having to do re-work, feeling like neither you nor your peers truly know what's going on or how to perform the tasks assigned to you. This can be extremely frustrating and makes for a scary situation when your work is potentially high stakes reporting and not just an assignment someone gave to you and that you find faintly confusing. So, from our perspective, like a syllabus is to a course or classroom, a sound data dictionary is the touchstone of a well-functioning data team.

One of Us (Jared)

Jared worked on three separate data dictionary projects over the course of 6 years - not one of which wound up being completed. In Jared's experience, each of the projects suffered from scoping issues. One project was much too broad and abstract (XML schema metadata documentation of all touches of all data elements at all times for everyone!) and one was too narrow and idiosyncratic with an unclear audience (documenting just the data elements upon which accountability reports depend).

Despite these shortcomings, the research team developed an informal data dictionary through a shared Google spreadsheet that captured the information relevant to data analysts related to commonly used data elements. More and more users outside of the data analyst role were given access to and contributed to the effort - leading to the organic development of a useful data dictionary that sparked many interesting conversations about data quality along the way.

In this way, the pitfalls of scope creep turned into adjustments Jared and his teams made to eventually get to the point of producing a useful and shared document that helped many different staff members do their work better together. This should be considered a win! This kind of iterative process is also another good reason to try to keep your expectations modest and to regularly remind yourself that baby steps count as steps.

Data dictionaries can come in all shapes and sizes, and scoping the data dictionary project can be a hard, but very important step.

One of Us (Wendy)

In Vermont, Wendy's teams first tried and then abandoned updating an outdated, legacy data dictionary. They found better return on their time investment by wrapping their updating process into a comprehensive Common Education Data Standards (CEDS) mapping effort they have to conduct in order to adopt the CEDS normalized data schema. By making this change in focus, they were able to elide the data dictionary work into their overarching strategic initiative of standing up an enterprise data environment (EDE) which is needed in order to support ownership and coherent operation of several large scale data platforms.

By working to integrate many (many, many, many) disparate data collections among several different platforms across the institution, adopting the CEDS model and definitions wherever possible, and only extending the model outwards for highly state-specific needs, the Vermont team is pushing aside years of deferred maintenance as they transition to a completely new approach to "doing data" at the organization.

At the time of this writing, the work is still in flight, but has been more than worth the effort to start. It's providing a structured means of exchanging knowledge, institutionalizing the standardization of naming conventions, and is beginning to facilitate the group in supporting one another through shared language and code builds. This has reduced friction among team members and boosted automation capacity for mandated, regular reporting while starting to promise the creation of slack in the otherwise overburdened system. This work has begun to create room for innovation in the group, something everyone, including leadership, wants.

These stories are food for thought. No one particular approach is going to suit all institutional needs, and we provide our reflections on these experiences as a way for you to think about what and how you and your team could approach this work.

Still, we do think that there are some guideposts for the work. Below, we share three overarching concepts we felt captured the main reasons why these kinds of products, and the work it takes to maintain them rigorously, are important for analysts.

There are far, far more than three solid justifications for curating your data dictionary carefully and extensively so others can use it.

But for brevity's sake over the next few pages, we'll unpack, in no particular order, these three:

1. Longitudinal *data management* requires well kept records so your architecture can be maintained, updated, and or migrated to new platforms and or used by new software as time goes by.
2. Being able to conduct *sound analysis* means you need to have a deep and precise understanding of the data you're working with or you run the risk of seriously misusing the data and coming to erroneous conclusions. You also need to be able to explain what you've done so others can understand the products you've shared. We'll introduce this idea here and examine it in much more detail throughout the chapters on methods 7.
3. Having strong, detailed documentation like a well-cared for data dictionary can *provide continuity* when there is disruption due to staffing and or structural changes. When you have thoroughly documented systems, standard operating procedures (SOPs), and foundational products in place, you can generally smooth the onboarding of new folks (as well as the departures of others not being replaced) and maintain continuity of workflow.

2.4 Data Management

Data dictionaries keep track of all kinds of fundamental information forming the basic elements of an organization's knowledge architecture. They can (and we think, should) document the information that developers and DBAs alike need in order to create space for, enforce rules upon, link together, backup, protect, and generally maintain the data that analysts and the institution itself needs to function and carry out their responsibilities.

They hold information like why collections began in the first place, and which reporting requirements datasets can (or must) support. They also describe when and why codesets (or option sets by another name) came into and out of use, which is absolutely critical knowledge if you're doing any kind of longitudinal work. More on that in a moment.

Data dictionaries that maintain background, like which elements from various collections actually are the same thing even if they're called something different, are invaluable resources[11] to those trying to link sets together appropriately as well as those who are hoping to create efficiencies in storage and use.

This is a noteworthy attribute because situations where data are not normalized[12] or standardized actually happen more often than you might think. "Normalization" refers to when you adopt the standards and structures of the normal forms in relational databases[13] in the relational modeling system[14]. Extending a database out to accommodate new data housing and reporting needs can be challenging when you don't have a unified, normalized data model that you can expand upon to meet these new and or changing needs.

This is something to think hard about because in the world of administrative data, especially at the state or federal levels, collections arise and change as responses to particular reporting requirements at different times. They are often developed by staff who may have moved on to new roles by the time you're joining the institution to use the data gathered from those collection mechanisms.

Good data dictionaries position you well to start the normalization and standardization processes where and when you can, if it hasn't been started already. If they haven't been started, you should try to start them as soon as you're able. This is another place

---

[11] https://indianajones.fandom.com/wiki/Grail_Diary

[12] https://en.wikipedia.org/wiki/Database_normalization

[13] https://en.wikipedia.org/wiki/Relational_database

[14] https://en.wikipedia.org/wiki/Relational_model

where the fellowship with the other stewards can and should happen. As noted earlier, sharing your documentation together and learning from one another is a great place to start. If normalization processes across data sets haven't happened very much at your institution, then this can be a perfect time to gather the data stewards together and begin the effort as a united group[15].

This is a particularly good kind of project to collaborate on because, in general, there are few instances where two or more collections are created simultaneously and their data normalized into a single data model[16]. This disconnection (some might call it "siloing" even) of data collections is an unfortunate hazard of the arena and creates serious overhead for all data work the institution has to perform with the many collections it is responsible for.

In recent years, one fantastic opportunity to do that normalization work is in the instances of large scale data warehousing projects. By undertaking such work organizations can, and must, take the time to bring together the people who know their data fluently. The collective knowledge each steward has is a key determinant to enabling integration and eventually interoperability of data systems across the institution and the analysts who serve there. Efforts like these can be arduous if documentation, like a comprehensive data dictionary, hasn't been maintained consistently up to that point. It can also be especially difficult if the stewards haven't been brought together to shape and inform the work.

On their most basic level, those data on where collections sprang from and when, the types, lengths, primary or surrogate keys, mappings to other collections, and codeset values, whether written down or held in a steward's head, represent the very bones of an institution's most valuable assets.

To this end, updating an institution's data dictionary is often no small task if it's suffering from considerable deferred maintenance. This is why it is more efficient and responsible in the long run for

---

[15] https://en.wikipedia.org/wiki/Knights_of_the_Round_Table

[16] https://en.wikipedia.org/wiki/Data_model

the organization to prioritize making time and space for their data staff to do this work on an ongoing basis together.

Considering all the audiences that must rely on it to carry out the work of the institution, it behooves us to incorporate this care taking as a regular part of our workflow. It also underscores how important it is to connect the people who do this work so they can undertake it as a group greater than the sum of its parts.

Incidentally, this is a perfect place to start when thinking about the larger framework of data governance for an institution because all rules and guidelines about how to work on and with an institution's data stem from what the data are and what they mean. Usually one group leads this kind of work, and who better than the people who look after and must use the data on a daily basis? More on data governance shortly.

In reality though, this kind of documentation rarely happens in an institutionally coherent and cohesive fashion.

That's why it's up to you to claw back that time and make it a priority in the daily practice of your craft. Make it a habit so it's not an extraneous effort. Here are a few ways you can do this:

1. Maintain your codeset values longitudinally. Always. Depending on how your current data dictionary is structured and housed (more on that in the next section), having begin and end dates for these values might be enough to do the trick.
2. As soon as something changes (e.g. a new reporting requirement adds or otherwise changes codeset values to a collection), make notes in the data dictionary's description area for that collection that detail where these changes came from and the effective dates. If there was a statutory change, add that statutory reference so others who come after you can look it up if they need to.
3. If changes happen, make sure they are reflected in any mapping or crosswalk documentation you need to maintain (don't make an edit in one place but not in others that it impacts). And don't keep this to yourself. Hoarding

information doesn't empower you. It disempowers others and presents a risk to the organization. Don't be a jerk.
4. Create a culture of preventative maintenance. Talk with your colleagues about why you think this is important, why it's good for the institution (and the team) to do the work, and try to create an ethic of collaboration together in your work to steward the data. Beyond many hands making for light work, remember that this isn't your data or your work ultimately. These are the institution's data and work and they'll need it after you move on to other roles. Take the character of stewardship that this work carries with it seriously. That's why we call this public service, right?

2.4.1   Sound Analysis: Grinding for the Good of the Metadata

As introduced above, keeping track of when and how codeset values have changed over time is absolutely imperative for doing good longitudinal work. For a particularly good example of what this kind of documentation looks like in practice, take the US Census Bureau's Survey of Income and Program Participation[17] data. They are a linchpin to myriad work across the US and indeed, the world. They serve as one of the most heavily utilized data sets about income and participation in government assistance programs so are a kind of bellwether for policy makers, analysts, researchers, and thinkers in these areas.

This collection has been going on since 1983, but like most collections, it has changed a bit over time. If codeset values shifted over the course of a collection's lifetime, and you don't know why or when, it makes longitudinal work really tricky to do well. Without this kind of information, it's hard to know when it is and isn't appropriate to collapse categories to try to adjust or account for changes in the collection across years. You also need this kind of information in order to know if you can drop values (if appropriate),

---

[17] https://www.census.gov/sipp/

or to look for patterns in the data that might indicate bias before you start crafting your more complex analysis.

The chapters on methods 7 expand on this information in much greater detail, but for the discussion about the role of maintaining metadata and in particular, the data dictionary itself, this is an important point because if you're going to be a responsible user of the data, you need to know what it can and can't tell you. You need to know what each element means, where it came from, when the collection started or changed. Those details tell you a lot about the steps you're going to need to take if you're going to use them responsibly.

For example, your data dictionary should capture if a collection came into effect in School Year (SY) 2013 (which is different from calendar year 2013 which is also different from fiscal year 2013 by the way and should be noted in your data dictionary) as a student-level collection. If possible (and there is space), there should be a note about expecting poor data quality at least in the SY 2013 (and probably the SY 2014) set.

Additionally, there might also be some notes about what types of tests you may want to do with a particular dataset before you run with it. For example, the American Institutes of Research (AIR) on behalf of the National Center for Education Statistics (NCES) recommend a nonresponse bias analysis if the response rate in an administration of the Education Department School Climate Surveys (EDSCLS)[18] is below 80%. This would be a good thing to note in the data dictionary for this collection if you administer it, along with a link or path to where a copy of the technical and administration guide[19] lives for more detailed info (and the R code provided to run the benchmarked scale scoring, by the way).

Ultimately, the metadata about what the collection can and can't be used for along with considerations you should make before conducting your analysis would be great information to add to

---

[18] https://safesupportivelearning.ed.gov/edscls

[19] https://safesupportivelearning.ed.gov/sites/default/files/EDSCLS_UserGuide.pdf

an overview section for each collection in your data dictionary if you've got room. If you don't, a link to where that information lives would be the next best thing.

2.4.2   Provide Continuity

Beyond its importance to doing good analytic work, a solid data dictionary can be the difference between smoothing out the on-boarding process for a new team member or making them feel like they've landed in a deleted scene from The Hunger Games[20] because they need to play 202 questions just to get the hang of the everyday data. Likewise it can be a shield that prevents you from ever having to hear "I have no idea, so-and-so always handled that and they've retired so I guess we could go through their files or something to try to find out". Trust us, that is way, way more frightening to experience than any Wes Craven[21] film. Fact.

Because onboarding new members efficiently is almost impossible without it (how do you do work on data when you don't know what it is in the first place?), and preserving some stability in workflow when you're institution should expect to experience retirements, carving out time to maintain (or build if you have to) a good data dictionary will be time well spent. As the Baby Boomers look towards the next stages of their lives[22], now is a good time to be thinking about this for those of us who will remain behind to carry the work forward.

Being proactive about your metadata management not only eases the entry for new team members but it recognizes and preserves the experience of the veterans. This is especially critical if your institution relies heavily on people who know the data by virtue of their longevity with the organization and there isn't much in the way of actual documentation.

---

[20] https://en.wikipedia.org/wiki/The_Hunger_Games

[21] https://en.wikipedia.org/wiki/Wes_Craven

[22] http://www.govtech.com/state/beating-the-brain-drain-states-focus-on-retaining-older-workers.html

If this sounds familiar, you need to strongly considering making a budget for taking those folks to coffee (or tea or whatever). Find time with them and start building a more accessible and digital means of holding that information. In an environment where succession planning is woefully lacking due to both funds and sometimes foresight, when those institutional fonts of wisdom decide to retire or leave for a new role, if you've been able to record their knowledge in a workable fashion, the disruption to workflow will not be as seismic or prolonged as it might have been.

This is also part of why a robust and living data governance program and the documentation that it entails are fundamentally linked to this work. By codifying your processes, the rules, and the mechanisms around them, your people themselves no longer bear the brunt of holding the data and information work of an agency together on their own.

2.4.3   How You Can Do It

While there are certainly open source platforms that you could choose (e.g. MySQL[23], Hadoop[24], etc.) to build your data dictionary with, it may be best for many institutions to choose more established tools and platforms given the staff (and skill sets) they have in-house. This could literally mean beginning with a simple spreadsheet file (e.g. Excel) if there's nothing for you to start from. Starting is the important part and using a tool that you know others can use too so they can collaborate with you and support the effort, will mean much more in the advancement of the work than the particular tool the work ends up living in for the long term. We've put a basic example of how you can get this work going at the end of this chapter.

The tool to start with is an important consideration because, at the end of the day, the institution has to be able to maintain what gets built and your work isn't only your work. You are a caretaker of the work you are doing for the institution. If you leave for a new

---

[23] https://www.mysql.com/

[24] https://hadoop.apache.org/

adventure and you don't provide documentation that a stranger could follow so your work can be picked up by your replacement (and hopefully they have similar skills and software knowledge to you) or you were working on the bleeding edge of things, you are putting the institution and the work at risk.

Now, this is absolutely not to say that you should shy from new tools or not be innovative in moving from legacy products onto current day means of doing work more efficiently or effectively. It's just to raise that it's extremely important to be conscious of the existing skill sets around you, often non-existent professional development budgets for many public sector organizations, and that whatever you build (or update) will need to be functional and useful for a potentially extended period of time to people other than you.

By all means, take every opportunity you can to innovate. Just be conscious that change may be slow and that folks with skills in the areas you need to really make a dent in the technical debt[25] present in most large public sector organizations are probably going to be fairly few and far between. Anything that you do should align with the core goals of your enterprise architecture[26] strategy (if there is one at your institution, but that's another conversation for another day) and should be reflected as part of your living data governance program.

All that being said, in the rest of this section, we will offer some of what we've learned and describe how that has been helpful to us in being good partners to our colleagues by taking care of our metadata. What we discuss here is absolutely not a series of hard and fast rules and they won't necessarily fit for everybody or every setting, but they are nuggets that we've picked up that we think might be useful to you as you make your way in the arena of public data science. We offer these perspectives as those gleaned from working in environments that must often operate on shoestring budgets (on a good day), that carry heavy workloads

---

[25] https://en.wikipedia.org/wiki/Technical_debt

[26] https://en.wikipedia.org/wiki/Enterprise_architecture

(unfunded mandates, anyone?), and are staffed with existing, long-term employees who are serving beside you.

2.4.4   Tools to Consider

We recommend that you use an established database (DB) environment that your organization already supports and which can handle larger datasets, permission effectively, and create reporting products (e.g. views) for easy access and use of the data. Your DBA staff will be most comfortable in environments like these and there are a few big hitters (eg. Microsoft SQL Server[27], Oracle[28], etc.) that are all more or less industry standard broadly speaking. These factors mean three basic things for you:

1.   It will be less difficult to get your IT colleagues to create space for the data dictionary if the intention is to have it live in a place they're comfortable and confident with supporting.
2.   It will be less difficult to get your IT colleagues to help you migrate whatever you've got at the moment into an existing environment and integrate it with whatever currently lives there (if anything)
3.   It will be less difficult to get your IT colleagues to help you make updates and schedule regular maintenance if it already lives there and can be incorporated into their normal workflow.

This is all to say, don't make life hard for yourself. You don't need Hadoop straight off the bat unless you've got the IT staff who can (willingly) support it. It's more important to have a functional, living repository than to quibble about the relative strengths and weaknesses of particular platforms. For more on why it's important to have strong, functional relationships with your IT colleagues, see Chapter 3.

---

[27] https://en.wikipedia.org/wiki/Microsoft_SQL_Server

[28] https://en.wikipedia.org/wiki/Oracle_Database

If you've got a robust data dictionary already that's on a regular update schedule in a longitudinal RDBM environment, then by all means, explore more efficient ways to store and work with it, but until then, just focus on getting the basics right. Get something that can become robust started in a place that can be maintained and instill this work as part of the broader culture and SOP of your team.

Focus on the process, the performance will improve after that and you can set new goals for how you manage these metadata.

If you start in a tool like Microsoft Excel[29] or Access[30], make a plan to get to a more sustainable environment within six (6) months. If you don't, you'll never do it. It's like fruitcake. Eat it and get it over with. Doing this work well is a team effort and you have to generate a culture of ongoing dedication to getting the basics right consistently. This often means setting a good example for others, understanding the work as infrastructure that impacts way more than just you, and not being mean to animals (or the New Kids on the Block[31]...even if they wear velcro or neon or lots of zippers or something).

If at all possible, map your data dictionary to a standard like the Common Education Data Standards[32] (CEDS). Picking a standard and sticking to it will pay dividends in consistency, transferability of work and data across your institution, scalability, and reusability of your and others' code in the long run when you're performing analyses. These facets of how you and your fellow stewards "do data" at your institution are all part of how you actually document and build your data governance program as well.

Plus, these tools can help with any number of things, including weeding out requests for data. If you have your data dictionary mapped and posted to the web, you can refer requesters there with guidance that if it's not mapped there, you don't have it. This

---

[29] https://en.wikipedia.org/wiki/Microsoft_Excel

[30] https://en.wikipedia.org/wiki/Microsoft_Access

[31] https://en.wikipedia.org/wiki/New_Kids_on_the_Block

[32] https://ceds.ed.gov/

can save valuable time for you and for requesters as they figure out what they really are looking for. It is also helpful for providing transparency to those who might not be as informed about the data your institution holds and have assumptions or questions. It also promotes transparency, which, in our opinion, is a good thing.

Once you have your data dictionary shipshape, the other major area of consideration for your group should be data's counterpart, the business rules that they work within. The following sections below focus on this other half of the operational pie.

2.5   Documented Business Rules: The Data Scientist's Handbook

Business rules are entirely context dependent. The logic and rules for how you collect the data will inform and define how you can use the data, but they are not necessarily the same business rules that will guide how you use the data each time you go to query it to answer a question (or build a model to do something meaningful and damned cool).

If the data dictionary is your syllabus, business rules are the technical handbook for how you actually get things done and operate in the environment. Your syllabus tells you what to expect, when things are due, and what you will learn. Your handbook tells you how you must behave, what you can and can't do with the tools around you, the procedures for solving problems, and what will get you thrown out of school (or work or wherever).

Documented business rules, along with your data dictionary, are the means by which you prevent car crash data management and train wreck data analysis. Your fellow analysts and stewards will have to come together around a (probably very large) round table[33]

---

[33] https://en.wikipedia.org/wiki/Round_Table

to pull this kind of documentation together (much of it may exist only in folks' heads[34]).

Many of these rules should be built into collection mechanisms in the form of edit checks or branching logic which would prevent bad data from being submitted in the first place. But, in an environment where data collections can sometimes be an ad hoc response to a study committee or lack adequate staffing to tighten the front end or back end of the established collection mechanisms to do this filtering and sifting, it is critical to have documentation surrounding the rules the data are supposed to follow and you as the analyst must follow if using them.

They are also the kind of rules that DBAs and Developers alike will use to set up things like referential integrity checks when data are loaded into larger, more integrated environments like a data warehouse. They include logic like, if one collection is a certified collection, while another collection is not, but they must be merged, use the birthdates from the certified collection and not the non-certified collection when merging the data sets because the non-certified collection doesn't receive the attention from the submitters that the one requiring certification will.

Your business rules encompass things like whether or not your collection mechanism can allow a value to be null or if it has to discard that record if that value is missing. They can be rules about whether a particular date range for dates of birth is acceptable and or logical for a certain dataset. Specifically, whether it is likely there is bad data if there are students being reported in an early childhood data collection with birth dates that would make them teenagers.

They can also be information about how a decision is made, like if scores are above a particular cut point, then that record should be coded in a certain way or if a particular characteristic present in a record at a certain time constitutes membership in a cohort.

At the end of the day, they are logical guardrails that must always resolve as either true or false. Think of these as the logic that

---

[34] https://en.wikipedia.org/wiki/Snafu

makes the data sets make sense as you're collecting it and then trying to use it. They are the checks and balances that even out our ability to collect information about the social world when we're gathering it through people and not sensors (and even sensors have been known to make mistakes!). They're the rules that help us know what makes sense in the data set before we use it. They are like a map that guides our way.

2.6 Conclusions

So, now that you've read all this way, let's take stock so you can prepare for your journey.

In our opinion, the work that it takes to produce solid data dictionaries and well-cared for business rule documentation represent some of the most heroic stuff you'll do in your role. Not because they are particularly flashy codeces, but because of the freedom that they'll provide to you, and to those who will come after you, to do analyses that could be groundbreaking.

We think this because they also represent key parts of a coherent data program, and should be part of your institutional goals for excellence and best practices in this area. But, they're never really done and comprehensive ones are mostly thought to exist only in myth. This was part of why we chose the Grail[35] and other Arthurian[36] metaphors for this chapter.

They take time, effort, and bringing together people of considerable skills, oftentimes of varying dispositions, and frequently from far corners of an organization (unless you have a unified data unit and function as a well-oiled machine. Again, #lifegoals).

That hard, slow work and those unique, memorable folks, in our

---

[35] https://en.wikipedia.org/wiki/Holy_Grail

[36] https://en.wikipedia.org/wiki/King_Arthur

eyes, do represent the stuff of legends. We say this because the work is bigger than all of you. It reaches back to those that came before you and it provides something meaningful to support those that will come after you.

All this might seem flowery, but it's what we've observed, so we're sharing it with you.

When you're under the gun on a high stakes analysis and you've got lawmakers, reporters, and your leadership clamoring for an answer, that data dictionary, those documented business rules, and the other stewards by your side can come together to do something powerful. They can help create empirically-couched laws, prevent foundationless laws from being passed, protect students or teachers by making you and others capable of harnessing facts, accounting for public dollars, shining a light on inequality, and upholding rules that protect the vulnerable.

These are just a few of the reasons we picked the metaphors we did over these last pages. In our experience, we've found those artifacts, the work it takes to create and care for them, and the people who'll undertake that effort with you, they are your sword, your shield, your fellow knights beside you so you can use your powers in the service of good.

2.7 Appendix

For those of you who might be working in organizations where there are no established data dictionaries, here is an example of how to get started on your own. Remember, the important thing isn't that it's flashy, but rather that it exists!

TABLE 2.1: A data dictionary you can start today

Table	Field	Description
DROPOUT_DIST	ADW_KEY	Analytic data warehouse identifier for entity.
DROPOUT_DIST	DISTID	ADW district identifier coded from P_LDS district ID
DROPOUT_DIST	SCHID	ADW school ID coded as a numeric unique only within DISTID
DROPOUT_DIST	YEAR	ADW year for spring of the school year coded as YYYY numeric
DROPOUT_DIST	SCHOOL_YEAR	ADW coded school year. Character. YYYY-YY
DROPOUT_DIST	CO-HORT_COUNT	The number of students who completed the term in the school as measured in ISES_YE

An Analyst's Guide to IT

3.1 Introduction

IT and its resources (hardware, software, and human), represent an extremely powerful partnership opportunity for the data analyst. You should care about this potential relationship because if poorly tended, your working rapport with IT (and the tools they provide) will hobble you. If tended well, it can free you in remarkable ways. In this chapter, we'll discuss some approaches you can take to build a strong connection with your IT partners and some reasons why you should make such an effort a priority.

For instance, once you join the applied environment, you are not necessarily the one who controls the tools you have access to, the versions of those tools on hand, or how and when updates or upgrades will happen. These tools can range from your data management and analysis software packages to the types of operating systems available. This is sometimes a penny that doesn't quite drop until you're face to face with an IT colleague who is telling you something to the effect of "sorry, we don't have that here," or "that's not in the budget," or "we have to take this to Leadership."

In this sector (like in others, but perhaps not as much in academia), computing resources are almost always controlled by the IT department. IT is responsible for the applications that collect, format, secure, maintain, store, and manage access to the data at an institution. IT is a very powerful voice in deciding on the tools that it supports. This determines the means and methods you and your co-workers have access to for analyzing and reporting on data within your organization. If you want or need new tools, IT will likely need to approve getting and deploying them to you.

If you have a problem when using existing tools, IT will likely be supporting you in solving it. They are more or less the people who provide the machines, environments, and software you're going to use to do your work day in and day out. In order to understand your data, it's useful to have working knowledge at a high level of how data flows into and through your organization. All of this means your relationship with IT is a vital factor in determining your success in a data analysis job.

With those elements in mind, this chapter is intended to provide you with a 30,000 foot overview of the average IT department within government, or the non-academic, applied environment in general. This also includes aspects of their perspective you should consider, as well as some of the concerns they might bring to the table when it comes to data and software. In discussing this topic, our aim is to provide some strategies that might help you build a productive, collaborative relationship with IT so you can leverage your data assets in sound, safe, and powerful ways.

3.2   Groundwork

To start, we'd like to introduce you to the idea that IT should be understood as the single most critical, underappreciated, often-times misunderstood, major piece of infrastructure you're going to encounter in your career. If you want to be effective in this field, and arguably in others beyond the academy, you'll need to come to terms with the fact that having a poor relationship with IT is like having a poor relationship with indoor plumbing. And we're absolutely serious about that analogy.

Sure, the "business" side of the organization is what the institution is supposed to do, right? And by "business" we mean the divisions and programs that do the work that the organization is designed to do — to provide value to stakeholders, not so much the operational or technical work that facilitates the business units of the organization to run in the first place (which is an immeasurable value in itself, but we'll get to that later!).

For example, if you work in state or federal government, the "business" side of the house would be comprised of units that specialize in certain areas of regulation, oversight, and or support for the folks they are supposed to serve, etc. IT and operations usually are comprised of the people who keep the lights on and do the work that helps the other folks be able to do theirs. So the operations people are the teams who do work like manage the money (business and finance offices), the equipment (buildings and grounds offices), and the software, hardware, and data it takes to support the organization today (IT, and increasingly Data roles).

Also, whether "business" and "IT" should be thought of separately at all from an organizational standpoint is a discussion absolutely worth having. We personally don't think they should be thought of as separate, but we also recognize that this is how many institutions have operated, so for our purposes in this chapter let's assume that in your institution, IT is a gatekeeper of technology and hasn't necessarily been understood as an integral partner for all things the business must do (and improve upon) on a daily basis. Which is a mistake (just saying).

In our view, the thoughtful analyst understands that IT doesn't just ensure that the proverbial traffic lights of your organization work and intersections don't get overcrowded. The thoughtful analyst knows that IT contains the teams who manage the equipment, tools, and permissions that form the roads and bridges of the organization itself. They provide the hardware, software, networks, and security for your institution. These things can be thought of in no uncertain terms as completely akin to the very electricity grid, the water and sewer system, as well as the buildings all around you right now as you're reading this.

Let's think on this idea for a minute because this might be a paradigm shift for some. For others it might be obvious, but for a moment, just honestly consider the following:

Ever tried to do work when you have no access to the location of your work? Say if it's sitting on your desktop PC behind a firewall, or on the network fileshare that somehow is not accessible, or a cloud service that has lost its single sign on capability with your organization's directory services? What about if a server goes down completely?

What about trying to use a database that doesn't have any documentation or mapping[1]?

Ever tried to do work when the software you need to do your work doesn't behave properly or isn't available to you at all?

How about when you don't even have administrative access to your machine to get to the tools you need[2] or your login expired and you can't even get into or use the machine that facilitates you to actually do your work?

And how many of us have pensively stood probably a little too closely to a tech colleague while they try to re-image our machine and we whisper not-so-softly to ourselves, "Please let everything be there, please let everything be there" while shifting awkwardly from foot to foot? (Hand wringing optional.)

Yeah[3]. Welcome to the desert of the real[4].

Understand this:

IT are the people controlling and facilitating your access to tools, data, and the very machine you might be reading this on. Understand that IT manages, fixes, and generally maintains the system that you work within. And, understand that most of the time, those people are entirely unsung, frequently misunderstood, and often blamed for things that are absolutely not their fault or even within their control.

---

[1] https://en.wikipedia.org/wiki/Thunderdome

[2] https://en.wikipedia.org/wiki/Bastard_Operator_From_Hell

[3] https://www.youtube.com/watch?v=gDadfh0ZdBM

[4] https://en.wikipedia.org/wiki/Welcome_to_the_Desert_of_the_Real

You see, nobody cares about the effort and upkeep it takes to maintain roads and bridges until those roads and bridges are out and you can't get where you want to go.

If you don't already know this, then know it now: IT is infrastructure.

No one applauds IT for things working seamlessly. No one writes them thank you notes for increasing the server capacity you're working within so your queries or models will run faster. Nobody gushes about how clean the network pathways are. Nobody expounds on the beauty of the fourth normal form they've managed to shepherd those data into so they don't bloat the system as ginormous flat files.[5]

This is folly, because IT folks are some of the most creative, thoughtful people you're probably ever going to work with. Think hard about how you talk to them. It'll help you as a person and as a data professional in a number of ways.

For example, many data analysts might be more highly trained in the statistical or measurement side of things, but IT has a wealth of expertise in software, coding, data management, and database solutions. Most of them have to use advanced mathematics and analytic strategies every single day on drop-dead real problems to make sure systems run and people all around them can do work.

Imagine if dozens and dozens (sometimes hundreds even; or in really big organizations, thousands) of people depended on you to not only get through a certain part of your analysis, but to get it right, and be able to turn it over to them so they might use it to do their own work on an hourly basis. That's a day in the life of many of your IT colleagues. Collaborating with them can greatly expand your skill set (and teach you a little bit more about the meaning of Zen...or the Force[6]. Probably both.).

Moreover, forward thinking leaders are beginning to recognize

---

[5]But everybody-EVERYBODY-gives IT an earful when they can't get into their email.

[6]http://starwars.wikia.com/wiki/The_Force

these facts and so, increasingly, IT is becoming a critical stake-holder (and sometimes bottleneck) for policy change or intervention initiatives. They are a collaborator you not only need, but should respect and make an effort to understand. If you do, you can lay the foundation for a very powerful partnership.

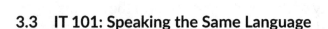

3.3   IT 101: Speaking the Same Language

Making sure you'll understand one another (at least most of the time) is a pretty important first step in any relationship. This makes getting a handle on some of the terms and jargon regularly used in IT departments a solid place to start. Since this chapter is about how to build this relationship, let's cover some language.

IT has a number of specialized terms, its own industry jargon, and entire business processes that IT professionals are trained to use to help manage their work. Oftentimes these terms are familiar, but in the IT context, they can take on an unfamiliar meaning. You've probably heard or used many of the following words and phrases, but here are what we think are some truly critical keywords from the IT lexicon to get you started.

What follows is ABSOLUTELY NOT an exhaustive list of words and phrases in alphabetical order that'll come in handy, but it's a place to get your feet wet as you begin to forge your new and or more functional alliances with your IT colleagues. We've provided some links to open access sites that will help you explore and develop your command of these topics, but please know that these are the floor and not the ceiling in these areas.

3.3.1   Business Rules

In general terms, business rules form the major guardrails that tell you what you can and can't do in your business. They are based in logic and always resolve to true or false. When taken in aggregate, they depict how a business must operate. In the context of IT and data, business rules provide clarity surrounding how data should be understood, where and how it should be collected, and how it should be structured for storage, management, and use. In addition they define and then confine appropriate data use and movement.

They establish how the data get created, how they get stored, and how they can be changed. They are formulated by the context for how the data are going to be leveraged and what you need them to do. Business rules can range from fairly simple (e.g. field X cannot be null [blank]), to complex (e.g. provide a Y [yes] result when the following 10 conditions in the data set, or referencing another data set, are met).

Taking a broader view, business processes are what create business rules, so getting a firm understanding of what the processes are that shape the work will go a long way towards understanding the nature of the rules themselves.

Be modest in your expectations when you're starting to explore what documentation may or may not exist surrounding business processes at your institution. For many organizations (private and public sector alike), attention to processes can be a very new idea. While process has long been a critical focus in manufacturing[7] and has become a key concept for development and refinement in knowledge work[8], don't expect that an organization will have a mature grip on business process management or have tools in place like a business rules engine or library.

At the end of the day, many won't have a central repository of business rules because to build something like this takes sustained, long term effort as business rules are dependent upon the scenario for which the data are being collected and what they need to do for the organization. That means there are a whole lot of them and they can change over time.

---

[7] https://en.wikipedia.org/wiki/Lean_manufacturing

[8] https://en.wikipedia.org/wiki/Lean_software_development

It may be the case that each collection, database, and data product has their own sets (possibly overlapping or aligning) of business rules. Business rules are often written as the code that the developers or DBAs in your organization used to build the environments in the first place and they aren't really documented anywhere other than there. Sometimes the only way to determine what the business rules in the data actually are is to be able to read that code (e.g. Java, SQL, etc.). Either learn to do it yourself, or ask for the help you need from your IT colleagues (another opportunity there for either your own professional development or to build some relationships with your IT friends). More on this topic in the chapter on metadata 2.

3.3.2 Change Management

Change management can be loosely understood as a set of governance rules and tools for ensuring that changes to software, hardware, and processes are approved by the appropriate institutional staff. The International Standards Organization (ISO[9]) 23000 has extensive documentation on the topic, and is a great resource that your IT colleagues might point you towards. Just like there are common data standards like CEDS[10], there are common standards that help many different types of work engender best practices.

Making a decision to change how an organization performs a particular function is a big deal, especially if the function is critical to the institution's mission, as data reporting can often be (e.g. produces a particular set of files for mandated reporting).

For our purposes here, suffice it to say that this is a very important process. Without clear governance, making changes to how you do a particular task or accomplish an entire workflow can be a complicated and even politically charged effort. Having specific steps and strategies for going about making decisions that will im-

---

[9] https : / / en . wikipedia . org / wiki / International _ Organization _ for _ Standardization

[10] https://en.wikipedia.org/wiki/Common_Education_Data_Standards

pact how the institution operates is very important for continuity, stability, and for creating the space for innovation as well.

3.3.3 Database

In the research world, because flat files are the most common form of files used in analyses, an Excel spreadsheet with multiple sheets may feel like a database. This isn't what IT means when they refer to a database. IT has something much more specific in mind, which is usually a relational database management system[11] (RDBMs).

Some institutions might be heading in the direction of a NoSQL[12] approach or a general data lake[13] already, but in our experience, this isn't that widespread in government yet, so having a grasp on RDBM principles will save you time and heartache when working with existing and or legacy systems. This includes such efforts as designing your databases so that all of your tables have one unique row of data and identified primary keys[14] among other considerations (ACID: Atomicity, Consistency, Isolation, Durability[15]).

On balance, the nature of many research areas that government/applied settings tackle use discrete administrative records, so RDBM infrastructure tends to be complementary to much of this work.

At a high level, a database is an IT system that stores data in a certain way. It is built for fast retrieval for the folks who need to use the data, and can be implemented in a number of ways. It is an environment that stores data in accordance with specific rules (business rules). It should conform to rules of normalization, or

---

[11] https://en.wikipedia.org/wiki/Relational_database_management_system

[12] https://en.wikipedia.org/wiki/NoSQL

[13] https://en.wikipedia.org/wiki/Data_lake

[14] https://en.wikipedia.org/wiki/Primary_key

[15] https://en.wikipedia.org/wiki/ACID

you will have a hard time maintaining the data, let alone getting ready to use it[16].

It's important not to violate the business rules of a given database or the work you're trying to do with your data will get really hard (and your database won't work properly/you'll break stuff).

Business rules can include logic that does things like enforce data types (e.g. string, numeric, varchar, datetime, etc.) and lengths (e.g. 2, 10, 50, 250 etc. characters in length). So for example, a given element (variable) in a database probably has some types and lengths associated with it so that bad data (i.e. data that are wrong or a mistake etc.) can't be loaded into the database and cause other problems downstream in the workflow. This is an important check that helps prevent problems for other operations with the data when you go to try to use it so you don't end up with situations like having values that don't align to the codeset of the element.

For example, you wouldn't want to load data into a clean data environment if an element like zip code was supposed to have a numeric data type (e.g. 05602) but some records contained string values for this element (e.g. o56o2 with o's instead of 0's [zeros]) because a.) this is dirty data, and b.) other operations for these data won't work because of that wrong value.

Other rules are couched in the logic of how particular elements are supposed to behave (e.g. you probably won't have dates of birth that haven't happened yet in your data set — unless you're doing cool projections or something like that) or how they are supposed to relate to another element (variable) in the data set. More on this topic is covered in the chapter on metadata, but for now, suffice it to say there is a lot to know about databases, and how good data administration and management help analysts be successful in turning data into information. IT knows a lot about this and you should too if you want to advance in this field.

---

[16] https://en.wikipedia.org/wiki/Mad_Max

3.3.4   Data Governance

The nature of administrative data is quite different from data used for research. This is because the ongoing analytics needed for the intelligent administration of programs and business processes require properties that would make it difficult to conduct research or evaluation studies and vice versa. It also holds with it fundamentally higher stakes in the lives of people on a daily basis.

For example, good administrative data use and stewardship are part of how families receive food assistance on time, medical services get billed at a particular rate, a child shows up as eligible to receive free or reduced price meals on their first day in a new school system, etc. The number of students receiving a particular service might vary day to day or month to month and an administrator or teacher might need to know the number of students participating in a service on a given day as part of their work to support those students.

These needs are different from those of solid longitudinal analysis. To do that kind of work, you'll need to take snapshots on a given date during a given timeframe over your desired duration.

With few exceptions, administrative data should be the most up to date version of the data you can get so that you can run the realtime operations of a particular system. However, data for research or evaluation will need to be a snapshot in time, and then frozen so as to build a dataset to perform analytic work that may take months (or years) to carry out. More simply, because the work is different, the data needed to do the work are pretty different too.

A few quick examples of how this manifests can be readily found in the questions you might ask of each kind of data.

Administrative dataset: This week, how many students have accrued enough absences that, by law, the truancy officer for that district must be contacted?

Research dataset: Between 2010-2018, what demographic characteristics are predictive of student truancy?

Regardless of this difference, both administrative and research data require good data governance.

Data governance[17] is, more or less, how an organization does data. It is the standard operating procedures (SOPs), the rules about who can use what data and when, the data classification[18], and the means in general of ensuring that an institution has high quality data in timely and efficient manners. It encompasses the business rules and change management processes of an organization. It's how an institution collects, manages, uses, reports out, shares, and generally puts data to work. Sounds pretty expansive? It is.

Data governance essentially lays out the road map for who can do what with which piece of data and when. Further, from an organizational lens, it is who has the authority to allow and be responsible for the use of data for a specific purpose, such as inclusion on a public facing dashboard versus a dashboard protected by role-based access.

It tells the institution how to treat the data, what it's obligated to do (and not do) with the data, and how to keep it in good order so it can be used effectively. Find out who your institution's data governance officer is and take them out for coffee or tea and make sure you know where you can find the data governance manual (if they have one, some institutions have more mature data governance programs than others for various reasons). If your institution has no such staff member or role and no such manual (sad to say, but this is pretty likely), read on here and throughout this series to start getting a handle on how you might begin that work or support it if it's in its infancy in your institution.

It's not necessarily reasonable to think that there will be a robust data governance program in every organization and this is because this is terranova for many places. Almost every education organization and IT department is grappling with data governance issues because data are starting to be understood as the critical resource they are.

---

[17] https://en.wikipedia.org/wiki/Data_governance

[18] https://en.wikipedia.org/wiki/Data_classification_(data_management)

As a result of this shift (which is arguably on the paradigmatic level), most business areas lack the expertise to be true stewards of their data, and IT is often left filling in the gaps with its own decisions and staff time. As an analyst, you want good data governance to ensure that it is easy to understand the data you are using and to help build capacity in business areas to become more data savvy. You and IT are perfectly aligned here.

This is important and living work, so don't be surprised if manuals, process flows, or data governance documentation in general have to be updated from time to time. Laws change, systems evolve, reporting requirements come into (and out of) effect, and analytic needs shift (accept this, make peace with it; your organization needs to be change adaptive). The long and short of why you should know a thing or two about data governance if you want to be successful and effective in this arena, is that it tells you what, when, how, and where you can (and can't) use your institution's data. Take this seriously. Build time for this work into your estimation of how much time tasks will take and fold it into making realistic assessments of the capacity and nature of the work you and your team can do.

Reach out to IT and try to build data governance within your organization together with them. Taking on this common challenge and providing extra capacity will be a huge relief to the IT department, and it will allow you to demonstrate that you understand and share the organizational goals of ensuring quality data so you can produce quality analysis.

3.3.5 Data Integrity

Data integrity refers to a condition of soundness that is facilitated by processes for loading and storing data that ensure errors cannot be introduced along the way. It covers things like the provenance of the data (where the data originated from) and data quality as well, which can rely on data integrity checks. Such checks are usually technical checks like confirming that all data elements that should be numeric are stored as numbers, text fields are the correct length and format, and categorical data are restricted to only valid categories.

It also does things like make sure that the hierarchy of the database's[19] model is maintained[20]. This means that it enforces rules so that you're not going to have elements without a parent record (e.g. how would you have demographic variables without a student identity record to hang them on? A student record has to exist for there to be demographic information about that student.) or have null values when those values are required fields for connecting to other data (e.g. how can you have an enrollment record if the school doesn't exist in the data set?). They determine how change happens to the data (and get propagated throughout) so as to ensure data fidelity over the long term.

3.3.6   Data Warehouse and/or Operational Data Store

A data warehouse refers to a specific type of database. Typically a data warehouse combines snapshots of data from different sources and stores them permanently in a common format with defined parameters and clear, documented definitions.

A data warehouse brings disparate data together to live in a single place so that they can be accessed or "queried" by data users (like your good self). In general, it will freeze the data in time, so unlike a transactional database, the warehouse stores attributes of the data as they were on a certain recording period and preserves them for the future. This is where the research datasets will live while the administrative datasets will live in the transactional environments. Different data for different work live in different locations.

Building these kinds of environments likely takes a lot of time as appropriate linkages between data sets have to be determined, primary keys defined and maintained, business rules documented and implemented (e.g. which data should be linked to what and

---

[19] https://en.wikipedia.org/wiki/Hierarchical_database_model

[20] In this case, "parent" and "child" records refer how a hierarchical database model is built, not parents or children themselves.

how?), and update procedures determined, documented, and standardized.

3.3.7 Enterprise

Enterprise is often a modifier used in IT to either describe infrastructure or tools that are used across the whole organization, or
to refer to a more professional grade of a specific tool. "Enterprise"
can also be used as a noun to refer to the entire organization.
For example, you may have heard this term used in a sentence
like "We are upgrading the enterprise shared storage system on
Tuesday." A sentence like this would generally mean that the IT
department is upgrading the shared storage system common to
the entire organization. You may also have heard something like
"We need to be sure to get the enterprise version of that software."
The use of "enterprise" here is likely referring to a more professional grade of software which has features available to make it
easier for IT professionals to manage and maintain over time, as
well as improve compatibility with existing software and services.
Enterprise solutions are often substantial investments and can't
be taken lightly.

3.3.8 ETL

ETL stands for Extract, Transform, and Load. This is shorthand
to describe the primary workflow for loading data from a source
database into a target database. "Extract" refers to how the command is pulling the data from where it is currently stored. "Transform" refers to whatever needs to happen to the data before it
gets loaded into its new home in the target database. For example, often there is some kind of procedure that must take place
before loading the data into its new environment, like renaming a
variable or perhaps performing a calculation (e.g. turn the value of
a variable into a percentage), checks the data using some form of
business rule (e.g. is the value of a particular element within a certain range? If not, discard the record as bad data), or manipulating
the element (variable) order etc. before it's ready to go to its new

space. The goal is to make the source conform to the target so that applications built on the target database can take advantage of data from multiple sources. "Load" refers to just that, loading those data you've pulled from one place into a new place. Often ETL is a matter of some discussion and can be a considerable workflow to define for the first time. This is because many factors have to be considered, like when the process should take place, how many resources it takes to run the process, other dependencies in the workflow (e.g. does the data need to go to one place or many places? Do other people or processes depend on these data? etc.). ETL is a critical component of how data flow and how they are governed. Pay attention to it.

3.3.9   Version Control

A system should be used to govern how you know and order which version of a product, or database, or file, etc. is the current version or the correct version to use. This can be naming conventions (e.g. V1, V2, V3, etc.) or date stamping, or record keeping, or a version control source management system like Git etc. This is part of how good data governance is done. More on that in later discussions on data governance, but for our purposes here, version control is an important exercise so that everyone stays on the same page, doesn't duplicate effort, doesn't use the wrong data for a product, doesn't overwrite anything on anyone, etc. It's a useful tool for analysts and software developers alike to elegantly track the changes to their code/results and rollback changes that did not work. It makes sure everybody knows what product to work on, when, and who worked on it last.

3.4   IT 102: Strategies for Successful Collaboration with IT

Now that we've discussed a little bit about breaking down language barriers between yourself and your new friends in IT, there are a few more things to consider when you're trying to make sure the relationship you're building will be a sustainable one for all of you (nobody likes a one-way street situation, right?).

Today, IT must identify and provide software, hardware, and services for users whose skill levels can range from "Why won't my mouse work?" to "Once I finish up the requirements for those stored procedures and you all can get those SSIS packages squared away, I honestly think we won't have to touch this except for like once a year to update a couple case statements and you know what, we could probably even schedule those update jobs to run if we really thought about it together".

There's a pretty big space in between those two types of folks and you, reader, are probably on the latter end of that continuum. This is a tricky place to be sometimes though, because meeting the needs of such different stakeholders is a tall order. The seemingly unyielding push to standardization in software and services provided by IT that many might complain about is actually an organizational strategy to keep these myriad tasks and partners manageable on a finite budget.

In organizations where analytics capabilities are new or not deeply integrated into business processes, the desire to explore new ways of doing things, be creative, and innovate can sometimes run up against the very real institutional need to uphold and maintain standard means of performing work on an institution's data infrastructure. These different needs can sometimes cause a disconnect between how IT and analysts think about data and data work.

For example, IT is concerned primarily with collecting, storing, managing, and protecting data from changes without authorization.

When IT is thinking about data, it's thinking of a valuable organizational resource to be managed and protected. From IT's perspective, uses of the data that do not involve IT are introducing
unnecessary risk to the security and integrity of the data if those
uses are not supervised and or permissioned properly.

And IT is more or less right about this.

Every additional user with access to the data, and every expansion
of access rights for each user, exposes the data to more risks. More
risk for accidental disclosure, deletion, or modification.

If you find getting access to data you need for analysis difficult, it
is important not to take it personally — IT is protecting your data
for you and you need to demonstrate that you can be trusted with
access.

At the same time, IT needs to understand that you bring valuable
skills to the institution that represent real and profound opportunities. For example, how can the institution do things like examine
where to put its efforts if it doesn't know what current performance is or what the past performance has looked like, let alone
why?

The knowledge and skills that analysts bring to the organization
can help address such questions and yours are the roles designed
to help make those data do something beyond describe a current
or past status for mandated, compliance reporting. You're there
to help those data tell the stories of what's happening out in the
world, what needs attention, what's going well, what's not going
so well, what's working, what isn't, and what might work better if
we did a few things differently.

You are a translator, a discoverer, and a creator. If you can work
well with IT, smart decisions powered by data can happen. This is
not hyperbole. This is the potential of doing data well.

With all that said, one strategy you might consider when you're
starting your relationship with IT is to recognize that they're trying
to protect you from yourself, to thank them for their vigilance, and
ask them for a copy of what you need.

When you are absolutely certain of the processes that need to be built and or the changes that need to be made, you should follow your institution's data governance process in presenting the case for developing those steps and or making those changes. Earn their trust, earn their respect, and they'll do amazing things with those data so you can use them well. While you are good, they can help you on your way to becoming great.

Armed with an understanding of the concerns that IT has in protecting the organization and keeping the computing machinery humming along, you can build a better, more productive relationship with them. This next section will help you think about strategies you can try to ensure that your analytics projects are more successful and run more smoothly.

3.4.1 Bring IT in From the Beginning

If you can, consult with IT at the earliest stages of your analytics or analysis project. This can be an informal or a formal collaboration, but doing so can save you a lot of hassle. IT may have a storage or data access solution you can use to save time and energy up front. Remember, these are the people that are facilitating, supporting, and working with data already. Even if they aren't the ones running the numbers, they know who is. You should probably know who that is too since you don't want to repeat something they've already done and duplicate/waste time and effort[21].

This early outreach can be especially critical when it comes to exploratory work that you're not quite sure is going to yield something fruitful that you'll want to repeat. Fail quickly and then try something else. Also, expressing your needs by describing your desired results or the desired states of particular resources might help IT understand what you're hoping to do more quickly.

By collaborating from an early stage, they can help you think through possible avenues and help you make good use of your

---

[21] http://www.encyclopedia.com/humanities/dictionaries-thesauruses-pictures-and-press-releases/circumlocution-office

time exploring potential solutions. This partnering can also help you avoid stepping on toes (who's working that cool project again?), do bad math, or generally put yourself in a tough spot with other staff/stakeholders with the analysis you're trying to do.

Plus, if you don't want to torpedo your fledgling relationship with your IT colleagues (folks you'll also have to work with a whole lot more as you establish yourself in your role in the organization as a data user) you probably don't want to engineer surprises for them before they know you and wouldn't mind eating lunch together (or at least going and getting coffee at the same time in the same space with you).

3.4.2   Play Up the Cool Factor

Most IT departments are used to dealing with routine tasks like repairing workstations or updating network software. Analytics projects generally require a more specialized set of software/skills/tools that are new and most likely interesting to IT staff.

These are really talented, intelligent people that you're working with here, so play your cool new project up — it's a chance for you and IT to do something shiny and exciting within the organization together and to help show that IT is not just there to help you reset your passwords.

This is also where you can start showing them your value and that you're not going to just be a toddler with sticky hands reaching for their databases. Be a partner, not a PITA[22]. They're smart and you are too; do something meaningful with those facts.

One of Us (Jared)

When he was working at the Wisconsin Department of Public Instruction, Jared initially placed a lot of burden on IT as he was

---

[22] https://www.urbandictionary.com/define.php?term=pita

learning the ropes - how data was organized, how SQL worked, and how to configure his computer to query data directly into his statistical software etc. During a remodel of their offices, he shared a cubicle(!) with an analyst from IT for about 9 months. They were revamping the public data download files in IT at the time and Jared took the opportunity to learn about the business rules and QA process that went into producing the published student performance data like AP participation, graduation, and student discipline rates.

IT was hoping to see greater adoption of the public data files. To try to help, Jared proposed and started working on a project, a precursor to ACS-ED Maps[23], that displayed public data files in an interactive mapping tool online.

Because of this alignment of interests - IT's interest in driving use of the data and Jared's interest in only publishing the most accurate data - they began a collaboration that helped them all rethink some of the organization of the data and simplify the production of download files while increasing their accuracy. Jared got a crash course in data warehouse architecture and the business rules and IT got a public facing application built on-top of the data to demonstrate to the public built on top of our data architecture. "Win-win" just about covers it.

3.4.3 Get Creative with Resources

There are mannnnnyyyyy ways to stretch a budget (which you'll need to do in the public sector/government). So many, we're actually going to dedicate a whole volume to sustainability in your analytics efforts, but for here, try these few ideas to get you started in thinking creatively about what you've got on hand. You'll need to be resourceful to be successful here, because resources are often in short supply. Make "challenge accepted" your mantra.

3.4.3.1   Reduce, Reuse, Recycle

First, IT departments and purchasing rules can make acquiring software or hardware that you need a slow process. You could also choose the open source route and skip the purchasing process altogether, but this kind of an approach has to be balanced with the very real security and administration hurdles that opting for open source software often brings with it. Not to mention the industry standards you can and can't expect folks to come to the table with (e.g. lots of people will likely be able to write T-SQL or MySQL).

On the whole, it's worth exploring in your organization whether you have access to education discounts (or free versions of some software), and if your IT department might have surplus hardware that can be repurposed.

For example, when Jared was building the Wisconsin Dropout Early Warning System (DEWS), his workstation did not have sufficient RAM or CPU power to test the predictive analytic models in a reasonable timeframe. He asked his IT colleagues if he could borrow a departing co-workers PC to have extra horsepower for long-running computations. His institution's IT team allowed him to delay their repurposing process for a few weeks and he was able to put a Linux operating system on it and complete his analyses.

After the success of this project, he worked collaboratively with his IT colleagues to acquire an analysis server for long-running computations, which they built together out of repurposed webservers. BOOM. Processing power on a shoestring!

3.4.3.2   Systematic Professional Development - Guerilla Style

Without a budget for professional development, Wendy worked with her unit to create personalized professional development plans for each of her team members that aligned to their internal annual and long-term strategic plans (also developed collaboratively with her team and revisited on a bi-annual basis).

By leveraging the best that today's (pretty darn amazing) MOOCs have to offer and providing one of the only things she could (protecting some of her team's time each week), the unit set to work sunsetting legacy systems and processes while learning and simultaneously, actively standing up industry standard SQL Server, Power BI, and Jupyter notebook infrastructure in the effort to automate data management and reporting workflows where they could.

This ongoing process has not only begun to free up team capacity for more value-added projects to date, but it is on its way to empowering program staff members to get their hands dirty with their data through an effort to provide interactive dashboards the team creates for them, all at the low, low cost of free (other than team time and software licensing).

More on strategies like this later, but for now, get accustomed to approaching resources in a creative fashion[24]. They are precious few and far between.

3.4.4   Use Their Processes and Procedures to Get it Right

IT is responsible for securing and controlling access to Personally Identifiable Information (PII) in your organization. They know a thing or two about configuration and data security and privacy protocols. Establishing shared standards with them so everyone can do their jobs well and together, will go miles for sustainability in your processes and in your effort to create and maintain infrastructure.

When you are making analytic tools for end-users in the organization, don't reinvent the wheel on authentication and protecting PII. If you need to set up authentication or store PII, bring IT in and talk through your application and your needs with them. They may ask you to rework some things (or jump in and do it together with you!) — but having standardized procedures for protecting PII is better across the organization and it is SAFER too. Less risk to data = less risk to the organization. This is important.

---

[24] https://en.wikipedia.org/wiki/MacGyver

3.4.5   Build Informal and Formal Channels of Communication

It's helpful to set up both formal and informal meetings with key IT staff. Information sharing is vital to organizational coherence and cohesiveness and should be integrated into larger governance processes so as not to duplicate or silo effort.

What kind of shape this takes is probably dictated by the culture of your organization, but all told, try to reach across the divide and build some bridges, so to speak. If they have to be ones that are made in formal meetings, so be it. If they can be looser, more collegial ones over a cup of coffee or banter about what happened in the last episode of a shared TV show, even better. The point is to connect, whichever way works best for your environment.

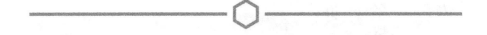

3.5   Conclusion - What to Take Away From This Chapter

In a sense, IT is a natural ally for an analyst, as you are often trying to build tools and services that cut across silos within your organization. This gives you both a unique perspective on the value of standardizing procedures and processes, and an intuitive alliance over why exceptions to the rule can cause problems later on.

An important way to support your relationship with IT is to always approach problems from this enterprise perspective — even when it may slow down a particular implementation or task. You aren't engaging in a research project for yourself, rather your work is to institutionalize organizational learning and that is an enterprise-level task. Organizational learning starts slow, but if you build it into enterprise processes, it will accelerate and you will be doing more research faster in the long run. Take this path. Taking the long, large view in this area of work will pay dividends. Learn their language, because it'll help you understand your environment and make the most of the tools and talented colleagues you'll be working with.

Demonstrating that you value the standardization of processes and adoption of common frameworks (e.g. DAMA and DMBOK, etc.) across the organization and being an advocate or ally for these procedures with the business areas you work with can help build your reputation and the reputation of IT simultaneously, while increasing the internal pressure to adopt standard business processes.

This will make your life as an analyst easier, not just because it smoothes institutional friction, but because it helps create a culture of data quality and data use. It creates an environment where data are understood as the critical resource they are, where they are respected as such, afforded with the support they need. Likewise, it supports the people who do the work of collecting, maintaining, and using them in sound ways being recognized for what they bring to the institution— as the mechanics, translators, artists, engineers, and the scientists they are, whether of the computer or social variety. IT and analysts can become a powerful team. Take the time to help make that relationship into the kind they write books about. You might just change the conversation in your field while you're doing it.

CHAPTER 4

Data Requests: You Can Make Them Useful (we swear)

4.1 Introduction

If your organization collects and uses data, chances are you are going to receive a lot of requests for those data. These kinds of requests can be internal or external, collaborative, or combative, and if you're on a team that's responsible for extracting, preparing, and or delivering on these kinds of requests, sometimes they can feel like a chore. They can even become the thing you have to do before you can dig in and answer your own questions with those data, and that can grate on folks.[1]

While thinking about data requests like a burden is tempting, it can obscure the vital role that they actually play in a data-driven organization. We say this because these kinds of tasks can serve as a strategic way to improve your data systems, create capacity to use data in your organization, and build data governance structures[2] that reflect the needs of your institution. If we shift our orientation to these kinds of workflows from one wherein we see them as additional, unplanned work that prevents us from doing our "real job", to one where we see them as an opportunity to explore and prep data sets that could be used in myriad other ways, we can

---

[1]Others have written articles on how to handle data requests addressing the technical, organizational, and political concerns. See for example: `https://slds.grads360.org/#communities/pdc/documents/15117`

[2]`https://studentprivacy.ed.gov/resources/issue-brief-data-governance-and-stewardship`

appreciate them as exercises in enabling data optimization (check out Public CIO's special report titled "Data: The New Currency" here[3] for more on data maturity models).

The difference in this orientation matters because an organization that values data usually establishes norms that decisions get made after consulting agreed-upon objective measures. One of the challenges such places face is building the capacity to gather, interpret, and act upon data in all of their business areas. In your institution, business areas may be organized around a number of functions, but they will range from content areas such as curriculum and instruction, assessment, or wellness and community engagement, to operational and regulatory functions like accountability, performance monitoring, IT, HR, and finance. All of these areas of the organization, as a public entity, will potentially be faced with requests for their data.

Given these conditions, we suggest that data requests shouldn't be viewed as simply more unplanned work (trust us, we know how hard this shift in perspective is...some of us are still working on it). We say this because these kinds of requests can be a vital part of the bootstrapping process for building a culture of data use in your organization because they're an issue related to data that affects the entire place. Everyone is likely to feel this pressure at some point in the year, and wouldn't it be nice if this pressure wasn't so hard to ease? This is part of why we think this is an issue the entire institution could get behind.

4.2   Taking a different perspective

In changing our view of the data request from unexpected additional task to an enterprise-wide rallying point, we're recognizing

---

[3] https://drjdbij2merew.cloudfront.net/PCIO/PCIO_Mag_Fall2016.pdf

that internal and external stakeholders requesting data are potential allies in this process — by requesting those data, they have bought into (at least in some way) the ethos of data-driven decision making. They are trying to use data, but lack the specific capacity or the data collection themselves to implement it — so they are requesting data from you and your team (politely or otherwise).

When we think about internal and external stakeholders, here are some examples that we've encountered:

Internal	External Stakeholder	External Other
Internal research staff	Governor's office	Press
Accountability staff	State legislature	University researcher
Senior Leadership	School board	Students
Performance management staff	Support Service Agencies	Advocacy organizations
Curriculum and Instruction staff	(healthcare, foster	
Programmatic staff	services, etc.)	

FIGURE 4.1: Internal and External Stakeholders

Any of these stakeholders could be looking for data on any given day of the week (this is usually more frequent during legislative session[4], however). Having to respond to those data requests serves as a pivotal impetus in the effort to become more data-oriented in general.

If stakeholders are told to use data, but then not given access to the data, they will rightfully conclude that the "data-driven" verbiage is smoke and mirrors. If they are given access to data, but the data are poorly organized and unclear, they will rightfully conclude that their organization is not serious about making the changes necessary to treat and use data as the valuable assets they are. And, if they are given access to the data, but they are made to feel like outsiders or are excluded by patronizing or hostile language, they will conclude that there is no room for their input in the push to become data-driven.

Data requests are a, if not the, vital link between the data collection and reporting operation in an organization and the business areas

---

[4]https://en.wikipedia.org/wiki/Legislative_session

and stakeholders that carry out the work of the institution. If this link is broken, or decays, or is an unwelcome environment, then the data-driven mission will become isolated to just collection and reporting, and business-as-usual-with-no-data will persist across the organization. People probably also won't exactly want to sit with you at lunch either.

In all seriousness, from an operational standpoint, this is a risky place to be. Funding for data collections and data systems will grow constrained as business areas protect their funds from being used on a project they see no value or benefit in. External stakeholders will become suspicious of the accuracy in the institution's data collections and reports. Competing parallel data collection processes and systems will be built for specific stakeholders to fit their needs. And the whole thing will descend into chaos[5].

So, while it may feel like a chore, it's much closer to critical maintenance like an oil change than it is to polishing your shoes. If you don't do it, eventually things will slowly, then rapidly start failing in your organization.

Think about it this way, data are some of the most critical assets around. You know this, but if you hoard them jealously and see providing them to others who need them as nothing but an onerous task, those others will find little value in you and the data, as they have no access to them (and don't particularly enjoy working with you. So eat lunch by yourself, why don't you?). If your colleagues (and leadership) don't see value in you and your work, that's not a great space to occupy, now is it?

Why not choose a different path and perspective? Because unlike an oil change, you can build automated processes and tools to increase the volume of data requests you fill and decrease the staff time required for them.

That groundwork will help them become less burdensome than they might seem at first. If you feel overwhelmed with the data requests, it's time to look at your policy, your processes, and your technology and ask what you could be doing better — not ask

---

[5] https://en.wikipedia.org/wiki/The_Road

how you can keep those stakeholders from caring about your organization's data.

Another reason you need to automate and streamline the process is that each data request is an opportunity for mistakes to occur. Manual processes and even manual touchpoints are places where we introduce risks in the production process. This includes risk of data to be accidentally disclosed, individuals to be accidentally identified, or inaccurate and unaudited figures to be accidentally released to the public. We use "accidentally" a lot in that last sentence because it's been our experience and is our assumption that we all try very hard to do solid work. When that work is frequently manual though, an accident is essentially inevitable as even the best of us make mistakes.

Automation and defined workflows and processes are one way to defend against these events occuring. While this chapter is not about security and privacy per se, it is still important to mention that a well-designed data request, compilation, and release process, including reviews, is the best way to mitigate potential risks from data sharing.

The rest of this chapter establishes a framework for evaluating data requests and recommendations for how to build tools and business processes to address each of the different kinds of requests your organization receives. Let's start with the framework, and reveal that not all data requests are created equal.

------------------------------ ⬡ ------------------------------

4.3   Prioritizing and Triaging Requests: Data Governance to the Rescue

First and foremost, while probably needless to say (but we're going to say it anyway), no personally identifiable information (PII) or sensitive data should ever be shared without having an appropriate data sharing agreement in place with the requestor/requestor's institution (sometimes such agreements are called a Memorandum of Understanding or a Data Use Agreement or data sharing is covered by some other kind of contractual relationship). We'll discuss this more later.

Next, let's be honest, your time is finite.

The time you have in your work week to fulfill data requests is a limited resource. In the presence of scarcity, you might normally introduce market forces — and some agencies do use a fee structure (and instate a fee waiver process) to help manage requests. But, in absence of that, you need an organizing framework to prioritize and manage data requests.

This prioritization work (and ultimately approval and rejection of data requests) as well as the safeguarding of PII and data privacy, are all part of data governance. In fact, one of the best and most tangible data governance activities your organization can work on — if you haven't already yet — is establishing a prioritization and approval process that balances the competing pressures on limited resources, the desire to use data, and the need to protect and safeguard personally identifiable information (PII).

Building out formal, documented rules that help the organization make consistent decisions about priorities and how data request work is managed creates order and transparency. If your workplace doesn't have this up and running, the Privacy Technical Assistance Center[6] (PTAC) is a great resource at the federal level to help. For our purposes here, we'll provide you some guardrails we hope you find helpful.

Generally, to identify the priority level of a given request, you need to assess the requestor and their relationship to your organization. If you haven't done so already, take some time and review the chapters on metadata and bureaucracy — after you take a look, you should have the tools you need to organize your requestors into some basic categories.

As a brief refresher, internal requestors are people within your

---

[6] https://studentprivacy.ed.gov/

agency or organization requesting data, or people contracted or working directly for your agency requesting data. Yes, these count and internal requests are one of the most vital functions you can perform to provide immediate value to your colleagues (and your institution), so streamlining and optimizing for them is critical to the sustainable flow and mitigation of risk in the regular data production operations in the organization.

This means if your Special Education department has contracted with a local university to evaluate a pilot program, you should treat data requests from the university pertaining to that project as internal requests.

Similarly, it has been our experience that an external requestor should be considered a stakeholder (and thus given priority) if they are working in alignment with your agency toward some common goal. For example, if a county child welfare agency is putting together a proposal for additional funding for school-based healthcare services, which your agency supports, then the child welfare agency should be considered an external stakeholder, not just a general requestor of data.

If, however, the requestor is a prominent national researcher doing an interesting study, but not directly linked to strategic priorities of your agency — this request should generally be considered a lower priority due to the lack of immediate and direct benefit to the organization. Again, if the researcher is looking for PII or sensitive data, this type of request should be handled through your institution's review process for such proposals, as this will require additional resources beyond you if the work is deemed an effort the organization wants to participate in. Such resources would include your organization's legal team, IT, etc. meaning this type of request is a little more involved than those that may hit your desk looking for aggregate data.

So, on balance, as providing data or public records is part of the institution's obligation to the public, we recommend identifying strategies to automate and mitigate as many requests as possible by providing self-service tools or other techniques to reduce the effort required to fill such requests. This goes for requests for data that are publicly shareable and data that your internal stakeholders need to complete their work.

Incidentally, you may find that investing in the work of building good data documentation pays off really well here because if you have self-service tools with the documentation needed to use the data responsibly, you'll cut down on folks needing to ask you questions about the data they're able to access themselves.

Ultimately, we think it's good to recognize that you alone may not be able to make a judgment about the position of the requestor or a given request in your work queue. In fact, organizing requests and developing an easy to use framework along this line is a great task for an internal committee of cross-agency stakeholders as part of your data governance program. This kind of collective effort helps build buy-in and provides a voice to folks across your organization in decisions about data, creating a shared sense of responsibility for managing them as an organizational asset.

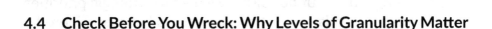

4.4   Check Before You Wreck: Why Levels of Granularity Matter

Some of you may gloss over this section because you already know this, but for others, this could be a lifesaver, so bear with us.

The level of granularity that a given request asks of you and the data will determine not just how you approach responding to the request, but it will also determine whether you engage in responding at all. Because of privacy law and rules at federal and state levels[7], certain data are protected and others are publicly reportable. This means that knowing when and how you can provide data in response to a request is critical. Having good documentation about data classification[8] as part of data governance can

---

[7] https://studentprivacy.ed.gov/

[8] https://en.wikipedia.org/wiki/Data_classification_(data_management)

help, but having a solid understanding of the level of aggregation you're being asked about by a requestor can be just as useful.

We think the most important thing to consider about the data you're being asked for is whether the information would be personally identifiable information (PII) were you to fill the request.

Unfortunately, depending on the size context in your state, the laws your state may have around data privacy, and how your organization has interpreted Federal law, knowing what may be PII is not always easy to evaluate. To try to give some general guidelines on this though, the data requested may contain PII when:

- Data are being collected at the individual student level (even with anonymized IDs)
- Data are being collected at an aggregate level, but with groupings or combinations of characteristics that have very small numbers of students (e.g. racial category by grade level)
- Data are being requested on a very narrowly defined subset of students (e.g. 3rd graders whose native language is Klingon)
- Data are being requested on sensitive student outcomes (e.g. special education status, free or reduced price meals status, etc.)

If the data set you would need to use to fulfill the request do not contain PII, then responding to the request is usually easier — gather and send the data, or publish it online. If you find yourself filling a lot of requests for non-PII aggregate data, consider whether you are publishing enough data online so folks can readily access it themselves. For example, data that would generally be non-PII aggregate data would be those compiled to answer a query like "How many students do we have in 3rd grade?" or "Which schools have the highest/lowest enrollment?".

Though not necessarily what we would traditionally think of as a data request, such questions will often be directed to a data request process. It is important not to reject these requests and to handle them carefully, they represent the most promising place to recruit new users and stakeholders for the data system itself.

We will talk about the strategy for efficiently processing these requests later, but for now, it is enough to say that you will receive requests like these and you should see them as an opportunity to do good work and build capacity across the organization by helping others use data in their job.

The most granular level of data are those at the individual level and these are almost always[9] considered PII. This is the most sensitive data you will likely handle and so it is also the most restrictive type.

You would not ever give this type of data to the public.

The only time you should share PII is when you are entering into contractually binding agreement with an organization that benefits/does work for your organization — and the details of what that means will depend a lot on the politics in your agency and the laws and rules of your state. There are some other very specific exceptions as well and we encourage you to visit PTAC's website[10] to learn more about FERPA in general.

Now, this is not to say that you can't craft shareable products from data sets that contain PII. To make a shareable product from a dataset containing PII, you will need to take precautions. Data suppression rules were created to avoid accidentally disclosing an individual's identity through their membership in an identifying subgroup or through the size context of the product you're making.

FERPA has a standard of the "nosy neighbor" which is not exactly specific — the data should be suppressed to the point that a reasonably informed person in the school community could not identify an individual student from the data publicly available. This isn't an essay about privacy and suppression rules (find that here[11],

---

[9] https://studentprivacy.ed.gov/training/b-cs-student-directory-information

[10] https://studentprivacy.ed.gov

[11] https://studentprivacy.ed.gov/sites/default/files/resource_document/file/ FAQs_disclosure_avoidance_0.pdf

here[12], and for the brave, here[13]), but needless to say, you must consider carefully, and seek review from your colleagues, about whether data needs to be suppressed or not when thinking about how to approach the request response process.

4.5 How to Respond to the Request

So far, we've established that data requests are not just about the data. They are an opportunity to show the commitment of your organization to treating data as the valuable assets they are and to using them as such. Incidentally, they are also a great way to onboard new analysts to help them get familiar with your data and data systems, while pulling their weight on the team in an immediate and powerful way.

One thing to think about in how you manage this work, is that in all cases, you should resist the urge to only supply the data. Taking a few extra steps with your delivery will pay dividends.

Sure, it's easy to dump the data out to an Excel or CSV format, compress it, and send it along the way (or send a link to where the data are posted on the web with no explanation of what they are or why they respond to the request). But, in doing this, you are missing an opportunity to demonstrate the skill and capability of your organization, and protect the data from misuse or misinterpretation. So document your data, your compilation processes, and share the data and documentation in an open format (Does "show your work" come to mind for anyone?).

You can build your data documentation up over time by adding details each time you fill a data request instead of trying to do it

---

[12] https://www.census.gov/srd/sdc/Massell.JSM2004.paper.v3.pdf

[13] https://s3.amazonaws.com/sitesusa/wp-content/uploads/sites/242/2014/04/spwp22.pdf

all at once. Data requesters may not always give much back to the organization, but one thing they will do is ask questions about your data! These questions are signals that the documentation is not as complete and as clear as it could be. If you find yourself answering questions about particular data elements or data sets, gather those questions and answer them in a single place and include those answers with the data when you distribute it. You'll be amazed at the goodwill you'll receive and how much you can head off emails from requesters trying to interpret the weird column names you know you shouldn't be using. Clarity is powerful currency.

4.6 Managing Data Requests

Now that we've discussed various approaches to responding to requests, we'd like to share some strategies for managing the volume of requests and the time associated with filling them.

4.6.1 Publish Data

Publishing data serves as your first defense in managing data requests and it serves dual purposes — it minimizes the amount of custom requests you have to fulfill as you can point to data that are readily available to the requestor and it makes visible the commitment to being data-driven as an organization.

The 100% absolute best way to be able to respond to a data request is with an e-mail linking directly to the data the person was looking for. The requester feels great, your agency looks great, and staff time consumed by this task is minimized. Of course, to be able to do this, your agency has to think strategically about what data to publish, how, and when. These are serious questions, with real costs, but consider the benefits:

- Provide open, accurate, and accessible data to potential users quickly
- Signal the organizational value of data
- Ensure proper aggregation and calculation of important indicators

In other words, if your organization wants to get serious about how to do data requests well — publishing more data needs to be one of the strategies on the table.

4.6.2 Collect Requests in a Single Place

The next step to bringing order to data requests is to funnel them through a common application and gather data about them.

You cannot manage what you cannot observe.

If different people on different teams field requests differently... well, now you have a mess. Plus, you don't know what data are important and useful if you don't know how often different data elements are requested. Investing time in creating a common request channel is a great way to get a handle on data requests and strategically tackle them.

Do you need to have internal audiences complete a 7 page data request application the same as an external researcher? No, because you can differentiate the information required by the type of requester.

You should funnel these requests through a single process and monitor the volume and type of requests your agency is receiving.

This is also an important data security step as well. While data security in and of itself is a topic beyond the scope of this document, it's a best practice to have someone in the organization be responsible for approving all data requests that send data out the door so the organization knows at all times what data are where.

4.6.3 Inventory Common Requests

Once you have built a common application and are collecting information on all requests, take note of the volume and types of requests you receive. Are most requests for the same information? Are you getting requests for data that are not managed centrally or difficult to acquire, organize, and distribute? Then it's time to gather that data together, and use the frequency of the requests as a reason to do so.

Review this inventory with your team. Show the results of this inventory to your leadership. Ask yourself and them — do we have processes in place to deal with these types of requests? What could we be doing better to accommodate this workload? Are we getting requests that help our agency and advance our strategic goals? Why or why not and what can we do to actively build partnerships with organizations who can use our data to help us?

This kind of information will be invaluable in helping your agency set its goals, build data governance work around the requested data, and make smart investments in data infrastructure to support your needs.

4.6.4 Automate Common Requests

You'll be shocked to learn that the most common data that Jared was asked to fulfill in his career was a student-annual file with some student enrollment, demographic, and most importantly assessment data. Within a few months on the job he could fulfill this request in ten minutes as it was so common and usually met the needs of 90% of the requestors his organization had at the time. He even had some data documentation that he would send along with the data that was useful. He was able to reduce the burden of this work by having tight documentation at the ready and by automating the production of this type of frequent request.

When you are doing this work, always be thinking about how you can automate it and how you can make it easier. Save your database queries. Save your analysis scripts. Make them easy to update when data collections are refreshed (make the date a variable). If you do this, then you'll immediately reduce the burden of the bulk of your requests, and if you make this a habit you'll build a library of custom data extracts that, over time, cover the vast majority of possible requests you could receive.

4.6.5 Use Request Approval to Build Data Governance Decisions

We've talked about this already, but much of the theory of data governance becomes real when discussing data requests and how your organization approaches them. This is a great opportunity to build up those data governance muscles. The reason is simple — lots of internal stakeholders in the organization want a say about who gets data and when. The above tasks of collecting and reviewing data request information are great ways to bring business areas together to discuss strategies for getting the most out of data requests.

This approach can pay dividends if done well. It builds a working relationship among business areas focused around data, and it places the organization-wide investment in data at the front of the minds of each business area's leaders (at least for the duration of each meeting). It also illustrates the real and ongoing investment that collecting, reporting, and sharing data requires if it's to be done well, and by doing that, it helps demonstrate the need for business areas to contribute to the overall project of building data systems through committing staff and resources where available.

―○―

4.7   Use the Data Sharing Agreement for Good

Here's another important part of data requests — while you are building your internal capacity to do them well and govern them effectively, you can leverage the requests themselves to get the analytic work your agency needs done. Now that's some Judo[14] right there.

Many agencies view data requests with skepticism because they don't find they provide much value back to the organization. This can be true, as data requests can open up the agency to risk if the partnering organization does not have sound intentions or aligned goals.

Unfortunately, education research is often not done well enough to yield policy relevant results or on a timeline that lines up with an education agency's needs. Other times, the research team fails to communicate their findings (frequently when they are negative or null) or when they do, it is not with the broader public in a way that can inform policy.

Still other times, some researchers have been known to publish their results, even as a press release without passing peer review and without notifying the agency of the findings or the researcher's interpretation of them. That's when you get lots of unexpected phone calls from the press. Nightmare.

The fear of events like these makes fulfilling fewer requests seem like the less risky strategy from an agency perspective. But, at least some of the blame for events such as these has to fall on the agency itself, and the organization's failure to manage expectations or set proper conditions on their data sharing agreements. Without accountability through the data sharing agreement, agencies are unlikely to get much of value back from external researchers.

Fortunately, the regulations around PII give agencies wide latitude in the terms and conditions they can impose on data sharing agreements. Through the data sharing agreement, you can also ensure that external research use of the data provides direct benefit to the agency.

The data sharing is at your discretion and federal law requires the agency to identify clear benefit when PII is involved. Use this. You can request research products in an accessible way (e.g. built on

---

[14] https://en.wikipedia.org/wiki/Judo

the software you use in your agency) so that agency staff can take advantage of them. You can also request research products packaged for the agency to take advantage of — detailed descriptions of data elements, policy briefs, and presentations to agency staff. Here are a list of items that you could consider requiring as part of a data sharing agreement that should bring value back to your organization:

- A report documenting all anomalies discovered in the raw agency data and an evaluation of alternative methods for addressing them (deletion, imputation, etc.)
- A descriptive report of the data requested at the level of analysis intended (e.g. a report describing assessment score disparities by immigration status across all schools in a district)
- An in-person presentation of the final findings to agency leadership
- An in-person presentation of the methodology and data cleaning steps to agency data analysts
- A thoroughly documented codebook explaining the steps to go from the raw data to the analytic sample
- The statistical source code used to generate the data and the findings (require it in the most common statistical language used in your agency)
- A fully reproducible script to go from source code to findings that the agency can reproduce and update annually
- Notification about the release of research findings[15]

Good research should produce these products anyway. If a researcher presented findings to you that showed some large negative effect of a program your agency believed to be helping — you'd immediately start asking questions that these kinds of documents would answer. It is in the best interest of the organization

---

[15]Note, this is for the agency to be aware of when and where the findings are being made public, not — as some researchers worry — for the agency to have veto power over negative findings. Some state and district agencies stipulate a several week review period for relevant staff to familiarize themselves with the findings before release.

to hold researchers accountable to do their highest quality work and to ensure that any findings that come from the data are trustworthy and reliable for agency decision making. Enforcing this in your data sharing agreement is a way of setting the standards for good research and a way to hold researchers accountable for the privilege of accessing valuable information and staff time.

We will have another chapter later that more fully covers the details you should consider when crafting data sharing agreements, but in the context of building a business process to handle a high volume of requests it is a key strategy to increase the requirements on those accessing the data in a way that advances the interests of your organization.

The barrier to most institutions setting these conditions on external research is one of capacity — it takes significant internal resources to monitor, evaluate, and enforce these conditions on external researchers. However, if the agency takes on fewer external research agreements, but deepens those agreements into partnerships that provide direct benefit to the agency — the volume of data requests to fill will go down and the value of supplying data and the quality of data supplied will increase.

One of Us (DJ)

As an external researcher, I've done independent academic research using state and district PII data and some contracted work for states as part of a research team. I've fielded a wide range of requests for additional value-added (so to speak) resources as part of the agreement:

Research findings written up in accessible language for lay audiences: One successful strategy has been to present in person the main findings and context, and then provide those slides as a document annotated with responses to the participants' questions and suggestions.

Analytic datasets, statistical codes, and documented data decisions, challenges, and fixes:

Program code should be clear and annotated, with any macros or shorthand spelled out, so that any agency analyst can follow the data decisions regardless of which statistical program they use. And, either within that annotation or separately, a write up of data decisions should highlight any issues encountered with the raw data files. These can include chunks of missing observations from some schools or programs in some years, or inconsistent variables or value sets overtime that needed to be reconciled.

Sometimes, agencies or major stakeholders request extensions of the research findings. Ideally, these are also specified up front in the data sharing request, so it's worth putting in some thought about this to be sure it's covered in the MOU. But some of this potential is only recognized as the initial preliminary findings are shared. It obviously depends on your agency and the research organization, but I've always invited agency staff and their stake-holders to make ad hoc requests at the findings stage. I can decline if the work would be too time consuming or is outside the IRB, but it can benefit a researcher in future work to be seen as providing more value where feasible.

Extended research requests: A common request is for disaggre-gation of the main findings by district (in a state) or schools (in a district). Another is to extend findings that focused on one student subgroup or subject to another: for instance, providing results by race in addition to socioeconomic status or by reading in addition to math. Some requests are more involved: such as, delving deeper into potential contributors or looking further back at earlier grades.

Bottom line is that it never hurts to ask. You'll get some "no's", but you may find a really good research partner along the way.

4.8 Closing Thoughts

Ultimately, by viewing data requests as an opportunity to build capacity in your organization, instead of seeing them as just a chore, you can build capacity for data users inside and out of your agency who can help produce knowledge that drives decisions. Your data should not be a walled garden that needs protecting. You need to think of them as a resource that you can grow and share with others by investing in their questions and building tools that anticipate their needs. By lowering the costs of requests and setting greater expectations on the return to those requests, you can move your agency forward in the pursuit of a data-driven culture.

So, while data requests are often framed as a burden and we speak with analysts across the country who express frustration at this work, at the same time they also express frustration that data governance is so intangible. Here, we've proposed reframing how you view both data governance and data requests — namely that data requests are one of the most visible (and valuable) windows into and practical applications of data governance.

In fact, if your data governance process on paper does not line up with the process by which data requests are filled — you'll probably want to revisit both.

We think that framing the task of data requests as implementation of the broader data governance strategy is the best way to move forward on both fronts. And win-wins are what working for an education agency is all about. It doesn't matter whether you start with data governance structures that exist and fit the request process into them or the other way around — what is important is that you make the connection and communicate the connection to all stakeholders.

Politics and Data Driven Decision Making

5.1 Introduction

As an education data analyst you've no doubt heard the calls to "drive decisions with data" or "use data for change." Organizations are making big investments in data collection, storage, analysis, and reporting with the expectation that those investments result in a more efficient, nimble, and dynamic approach to the work of the institution. And this expectation makes sense, these investments need to translate to shifts in how government delivers services, exercises oversight, and provides transparency.

In support of these ends, one of our most central goals as analysts is to enable positive organizational responses to findings revealed by the scientific method — policy guided by evidence and reality, not piloted by anecdote and impression. Arguably, this represents a paradigmatic shift in how government functions.

Such systemic evolution isn't driven by the volume of data or analytics available in an organization alone however. It is driven by the appetite for such transformation among the leadership. After all, the purpose of this analysis work is getting the right information to the right people to make the right decision at the right time.

To do this we have to accept some hard facts about the work, the first being that organizational change is often hard and slow (think about what it takes to overcome cultural and structural inertia.). The second is that the findings we uncover through sound data analysis are not produced in a vacuum. To be successful in helping the institutions we work within become learning organizations, we have to engage in the politics of the organization.

The belief that data analysis, or "evidence-based policy" is neutral and self-evident to organizations is a myth. The information you create through your work exists in a political landscape and data analysis is not a shortcut past deliberation, evaluation of tradeoffs, or balancing of competing interests. The role of data in shaping policy is more nuanced and maybe that's rightfully so.

We, like you, are scientists, each of a different discipline. We didn't take up our roles out of an interest in the political realm, but because we're passionate about the scientific method, data, and how technology can help us do powerful things to help others. But, we've realized that to do that requires a knowledge of both data and politics. Mastering each is critical, neither is avoidable, and this can be a tall order for many of us who prefer to "just do data."

To try to help you navigate this part of the job, we've found some approaches that have served us. We hoped that what we could share might help readers in some way because all three of us really wished someone (or three someone's, in the case of this book) had written something like this so we could have read it when each of us first took our respective jobs. So, here goes!

The rest of this chapter is a crash course in how to deploy the practices above in the world of bureaucratic politics. We'll go over what politics are, and why they are endemic to any large organization (government or private). We'll cover the key aspects of political decision-making that relate to change agents inside of a bureaucracy (sometimes called policy entrepreneurs). Then, we'll introduce the central role that information, and thus data analysts, can play in organizational decision-making. Finally, we'll wrap up with some key skills that will help you maximize your impact in your organization.

5.2 What Do We Mean By "Politics"?

Unfortunately for many of us, the term "politics" conjures up images of talking heads shouting loudly on TV. It can be hard to equate the hyper-partisan, sound-bite competition that we have come to associate with politics to the quiet, diligent work of keeping the public education system open, safe, clean, and effective — so let's reframe.

At its heart, we think "politics" encompasses the practice of choice-making that will affect the collective within the context of scarcity.

This reframing is important because there is a tendency to just throw one's hands up, lament organizational politics, and seek to disengage. Or worse yet, to convince ourselves that we can rise above politics and make "objective" decisions. We've each been guilty of taking these stances in our own way, and we can tell you confidently that they don't work. Politics existed before you walked on the job, and it'll be there after. If a decision matters, it is political, so if you find yourself working on topics with little conflict or deliberation, it might be good to stop and ask if that work is relevant.

For example, changing the font and logo on a website, deciding on whether or not to apply for a large grant for the institution that will encumber employees to manage it so as to carry out the work it funds, or determining how to assign staff to schools in a school district are all instances where limited resources must be allocated to achieve a particular goal. Deciding how to deploy or conserve those resources, and where, is an exercise in politics. Sometimes such decisions are easy with broad agreement, and sometimes Gary won't give up the Comic Sans dream and you've got a stalemate on the website redesign project.

Politics are the procedure for choosing "who decides".[1] Implicit

_____

[1]Who Governs? (1961) by Robert Dahl is one of the most important books

in our understanding of politics is some nod to representation and inclusiveness in decision-making — not many organizations are run by a supreme leader with unchecked authority. Most of what we commonly think of a bureaucratic red tape is actually the process of ensuring that multiple decision makers representing different viewpoints have an opportunity to weigh in on decisions that affect them or resources for which they are responsible.

When politics goes well it means that the right people affected by a particular policy, or set of choices, are represented at the table and the proposed action is debated openly and fairly by all sides resulting in a final decision that reflects a balancing of preferences from the entire community. This, like a perfect cup of coffee or a complex SQL statement that runs the first time without error, is an ideal — something to strive for; but also, in all honesty, something very hard to achieve.

You may have already sensed that the trade-off with this type of decision-making is speed. One of the most disorienting aspects of working in this environment is the pace. Political processes are much like tectonic plates — most of the time they creep along, sometimes imperceptibly. Then, occasionally, they break loose and in a few seconds, move a distance that would normally take decades or longer, shaking things up with an earthquake. Organizational politics are exactly the same.

One of Us (Jared)

For example, when Jared was at the Wisconsin Department of Public Instruction (WDPI) designing and building the Wisconsin Dropout Early Warning System (DEWS) it took time to work with all the affected parties, incorporate their ideas, and get their support of the project.

This process took an additional nine months after the proto-type was up and running, but it helped make DEWS so much

---

in political science and takes up the topic of decision-making authority and formal and informal power structures in municipal government.

better than it otherwise might have been. Because of all that stakeholder engagement, WDPI had strong messaging around the interpretation of risk scores, the consequences of labeling students and how schools should handle that, as well as how to deal with structural and individual barriers to student success.

The DEWS implementation represented a major change in how data were used to inform education interventions. The groundwork, and the politics of it, enabled critical information to flow to those who needed it, mitigated the risk of the public and other stakeholders of misunderstanding the tool itself, and empowered users to leverage the model appropriately to intervene with at-risk students.

At the same time, Jared and the crew quickly realized the method could easily apply to college-readiness as well — allowing them to help schools focus on preparing students for postsecondary education. DEWS and its college-ready extension were finished at about the same time, but DEWS was released five years before CREWS.

Why? The political work of defining and messaging what "college-ready" meant wasn't complete. But when it was, CREWS was able to be rolled out[2] swiftly and to much acclaim for how it helped practitioners use data to change their approach to their work. The timelines of DEWS and CREWS respectively are cardinal examples of the typically slow pace of political processes as well as the suddenness with which they can move when the right work has been done well enough to be ready for rapid deployment. We'll unpack why this is a bit more below.

5.3　Politics 101

If politics is inevitable, as data analysts we should embrace it. What are the most important aspects of political decision making we need to be conscious of? We think the most powerful and relevant to education data analysts are:

1. Policy windows
2. Credit claiming and failure blaming
3. Loss aversion and incrementalism
4. The role of information

5.3.1　Policy Windows

Policy windows are just the political science term for the "earthquakes" described above.[3] They can be created by legal actions, legislative interest, changes in policy at another level, the steady and consistent pressure from advocacy organizations, or from a new source of funding like a grant or philanthropic gift. They can be internal to your organization or part of the institution's role and work with external stakeholders.

Using data analysis to inform change involves, in part, being ready to serve policymakers with information when these windows open up. They also help organizations seeking to open them maintain the pressure and advocacy during periods when they are closed.

Policy windows can be frighteningly brief. Actions that normally take months can happen in days when one is open. The speed at which things can move (and that workflows are expected to move) during an opening can be disorienting at first. Over time, you should build up a reserve of resources and information you can deploy on policy issues should a window open up in that area.

---

[3]The term "policy window" comes from John Kingdon[4]'s textbook Agendas, Alternatives, and Public Policies (1984), a classic in public policy.

This will save you time, rework, and headaches when questions about your methodology for a particular analysis might be an area of interest for stakeholders.

As a data analyst, we need to learn how to prepare for policy windows, how to help create them, and how to capitalize on them when they are open. Having well-established metadata and documentation about the business rules used to compile a particular product during a hectic time like this will save time, energy, and capital in many areas. The end of this chapter will give you some key practices you can use to take advantage of these windows when they open.

5.3.2   Credit Claiming and Failure Blaming

The second piece of political analysis we need to be effective is to understand the concept of credit claiming and failure blaming. In essence, politicians (school board members, superintendents, legislators, governors, etc.) are always seeking to claim credit for ideas that are popular with the public, and are always trying to pass blame for unpopular ideas onto others who are not accountable to the same public.

For example, local politicians who signed off and adopted the Common Core State Standards found it convenient to give the credit for the standards to the federal government when they discovered local opposition to them — classic failure blaming. In places where the standards were popular, local politicians took credit for taking part in the development of those standards.

This is straightforward enough, but as an analyst you need to learn how to keep this perspective central in your approach to working with policy-makers and practitioners. It means monitoring what is popular with whom and actively being conscious about how giving credit and passing blame will function in that context.

This is a skill you must practice. One useful tip we have found is to think carefully about the constituencies that matter to those involved in the policy process. Constituencies are the people whom the person or organization serves or perceives that she/he/they/the organization serves. For example, while a state K-12 education agency ultimately functions to ensure the delivery of quality public education for children, the students themselves are just one constituency. A teacher licensing bureau likely sees teachers as their primary constituency, while a finance office may see district finance officers as their primary constituency. At local education agencies, these folks could be parents, teachers, the students, and sister organizations like county child welfare agencies that also serve similar groups.

In our roles, we've observed that understanding the different constituencies and their relative importance to different people in your organization is a helpful way to understand their motivations and incentives.

5.3.3   Loss Aversion and Incrementalism

These first two pieces — policy windows and credit claiming — are what explains a third key feature of politics: loss aversion. Most of the time, organizations are led by political leaders who are risk averse — it is harder to claim credit than it is to avoid blame, and avoiding blame is generally enough to stay in power. This often leads to incremental changes, saving 3-5% on technology services, reducing paper clip purchases, or maintaining services in a flat budget. It is good to build up a steady volume of small positive stories while avoiding a single bad story in this context.

Another, connected reason organizations move slowly and tend to prefer incrementalism is a function of how many people in an organization can say "no" and stop a change from happening. Gatekeepers[5] and or Veto Players[6] are terms that refer to people who have the power to provide or withhold access to resources, or to essentially say "no" and stop an action.[7] The "no" often comes from a place of loss aversion.

---

[5] https://en.wikipedia.org/wiki/Gatekeeper

[6] https://en.wikipedia.org/wiki/Veto_Players

[7] We present these terms more or less interchangeably here, because we believe that all gatekeepers are veto players since their ability to say "yes" or

The term "veto player" comes from game theory[8], which is a formal way of thinking about strategic interaction. The set of veto players is not consistent from action to action in an organization — some leaders like the chief executive always possess veto power, but other leaders only possess veto power around specific decisions affecting their program area or area of expertise.

To be effective, veto power has to be final and absolute. In practice, in many organizations, the threat of inaction and no formal mechanism of forcing action, creates many veto players by virtue of their ability to just not complete some work if they do not agree with it (or have loss aversion). The more veto players in a given decision space, the less likely action becomes.

Many people experience this kind of situation as frustration. While it is frustrating, it's an ironclad law of organizations. Knowing it, managing it, and managing your reaction to it are key. If you build relationships and coalitions, as well as your reputation, you'll find fewer veto players in your way, less loss aversion, and more success in trying to make the change you've set out to make. Most importantly, doing so means being open to ideas from coalition partners, being humble, and working together to creatively reach compromises.

5.3.4   The Role of Information

Finally, our last point in this section is about understanding the role that information plays in politics. Notice, *we did not say data*. Data are not necessarily useful in policy deliberations — but information most often is. Politicians are not data analysts and have access to many modes of evidence outside of data. Anecdotes, external studies, expert statements, editorials, and public opinion are all examples of modes of evidence that provide information in the public policy process — and all of them outweigh unanalyzed data.

The result of data analysis however, presented as information, has

---

"no" to something is a major part of what gives them the proverbial keys to the gate.

[8] https://en.wikipedia.org/wiki/Game_theory

a powerful role to play. This is because information reduces the uncertainty around the outcome of a policy choice. Uncertainty fuels inaction because of the loss aversion described above.

Information about the data analysis gives decision-makers more confidence about what credit will be available for claim and that there is a lower likelihood for blame. Putting information together to help reduce policy uncertainty during a policy window means that a data analyst can have great influence on the decision-making process, and as a result, the decisions that are made.

Think of it this way, for an organization, existence itself is sort of a miracle. Organizations are always fighting to sustain themselves, maintain funding, retain relevance, sustain their organizational mission, and so on. Given the cost any particular decision represents, organizations require both a minimal exposure to downsides — which would push the organization further toward demise — and a strong probability of an upside which greatly exceeds the costs associated with taking any new action.

In practice this means that if an organization decides to take a new direction, it will generally want to be reasonably sure that a) any risks associated with taking this action are small, and b) the minimum upside is greater than the costs associated with the change, with a potential for much greater upside in the future. Both a and b can be quantified if you have the right data to describe them, and this methodology for navigating institutional decision-making represents a space where data scientists can really shine.

If it helps, we think of it like this:

$$Pr(Action) = (\lambda_{benefit} - \beta_{cost})^{\frac{1}{time}}$$

λ represents the value the organization places on the benefit of a particular action. β represents the value the organization places on costs related to a particular action. The net benefit of a policy is discounted by the amount of time it will take for the cost to be realized. A net benefit that occurs in 10 years is much less appealing to policy makers than a net benefit that occurs today, even if today's benefit is much smaller than the one occurring in 10 years' time.[9] It is important to note that here λ and β are the organization's perception of the benefit and the cost, but not the actual cost. These estimates have uncertainty and bias baked into them, and depending on the organization, the more uncertain or biased these estimates are, the less likely action is to be taken. Data analysis can provide the information needed to help policymakers improve these estimates of values of β and λ.

We made Figure 5.1 to show how we think about this:

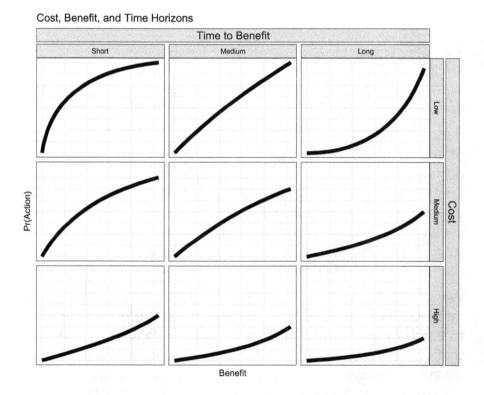

FIGURE 5.1: The Organizational Perspective on Cost and Benefits

Data analysis, then, is the process of extracting the information from an organization's data which is the most relevant to decisions

[9]This phenomenon is known as the discount rate.

the organization needs to make. Because your organization has likely made a big investment in data systems, information extracted from those data systems is likely to be well received in policy discussions. This creates an opportunity for your analysis to have real impact. The challenge is to use the data well and be able to communicate about them and your findings to non-technical audiences. More on this later.

5.4   Key Practices

So what makes these concepts relevant to the job of analyzing data?

Because information is so critical to the decision-making progress of organizations, the role of data analyst becomes politically important to the success of the organization in meeting its goals. This means even new data analysts (which we once were) can be given large responsibilities in the policy-making process — briefing senior leadership or writing policy options for a budget proposal for example (both scary if you've been with an institution for less than a year. Just saying).

We conclude this chapter with some key practices to keep in mind, but we'd be remiss if we didn't pause here for a moment to emphasize the importance of ethics in data analysis. The fact that you are reading this book is a good start. It is important to always remember that you have a professional obligation to think responsibly about the data you are using, the information you are providing, and how those you are providing the information to will come to use it as well. There is far more to discuss about ethics in data analytics than we have room in this chapter to review, but for now we can't emphasize strongly enough that you will need to be prepared to confront ethical challenges in this line of work.

For example, when one of us was still very new to a more junior role, there was a heated debate happening about district, school, and class sizes happening in their context. During the legislative session, outside researchers presented some work that did not disclose the methodologies and size conditions of the literature they were citing to support their position on the topic. These size conditions were far larger than the conditions under discussion in the context of the state, making the position of the outside researchers problematic for meaningful deliberation to take place among non-expert stakeholders, including policymakers.

When one of us made this clear, by examining the methodologies and size conditions presented in the literature review and then communicating the strengths and weaknesses of applying those findings to the in situ context, policymakers took pause. A position that had been gaining steam was checked by transparent examination and discussion of the data and methods themselves. As analysts, it is our role to be true to the scientific method, the data, and the methods exercised upon them. With specialized knowledge comes the responsibility to use and exercise that knowledge well.

This isn't about "always being right" but it is about always trying to do the right thing. We've found collectively that the following practices have helped us over the years and we hope that by employing them in your own work, you'll be better equipped to navigate bureaucratic, political, and ethical challenges as you meet them:

1. Humility
2. Repeated Engagement
3. Coalition Building
4. Reputation Management
5. Timing

5.4.1 Humility

We think humility is important for two primary reasons. First, data analysis work is hard. The stuff that is easy with clear rules and simple procedures has been automated. The tough stuff is left to us as analysts to do, or to invent ways to automate, and errors in the data or mistakes in our code are always waiting to humble us. Embrace this aspect of the work and seek to bring a "beginner's mindset" of caution and possibility to your projects. Doing so will make you less likely to make mistakes that threaten your credibility, and more likely to discover new and interesting approaches to problems that need to be solved.

The second reason is that humility is a ward against the trap of technochauvinism — the belief that technology (e.g. data analysis) is the best or only valid solution to a problem.[10] Education as a system still comes down to interactions between people. Superintendents and principals, teachers and students, state employees and local staff, school boards and parents, legislators and their constituents.

Sure, those interactions are regulated by laws and those laws are passed as part of a political process. And yes, data can be illuminating, but so can qualitative forms of data — observing schools, listening to students, and learning from the complaints and challenges that people interacting with school systems hear every day. The professional judgment of teachers, lived experiences of parents, and the day to day realities for students are important to keep in mind, and form one of the most important sources of data to inform your work and better analyze the data in your data warehouse.

5.4.2 Repeated Engagement

When you're presenting data analyses to decision-makers, you should make it a goal to get invited back to talk with them again.

Getting asked back opens up the opportunity for new thinking, for collaboration, and for real change. If you simply report some

---

[10]The term comes from NYU professor and data journalist Meredith Broussard who has written many excellent articles and a book on the societal risks of an overreliance on data analysis without incorporating broad perspectives. https://merbroussard.github.io/about/

information and decision makers move on in the process without any new questions or new ideas — then consulting the analyst was more pro forma than a valid attempt at data-driven decision making. To influence an organization then is to be useful, and the surest sign that your work has utility is getting asked to come back and join the conversation again.

Your skill with data gets you in the door. Integrity, accuracy, skilled communication, and a collaborative mindset get you another invitation. Keeping an open mind and working with others in your organization is the best way to build relationships, accumulate knowledge, and develop the intuition and insight that will make your analysis even better. No work is so good that it can make change on its own. Folks have to want to hear you before they'll listen to the work. Having integrity, ensuring good communication, being invested in accuracy, and practicing a collaborative mindset — those things add up to getting heard in our experience.

5.4.3 Coalition Building

If you are presenting results from an analysis and you look to your left, then look to your right, and no one is standing beside you, that might be a bad sign.

Sometimes as data analysts we can have an impulse to work solo; to independently pursue the "truth" in the data, and to present our results fully formed after we've done all the statistical modeling we can. Indeed, academia encourages us to work alone and to shine alone. That's the way to get ahead, right?

In the applied environment, conducting work that way not only risks getting it wrong (much of the information that gives meaning and interpretation to the data lies outside of the data warehouse) but it also shuts us out from collaborating with others to build better processes, catch more mistakes, ask better questions, and come up with more creative ideas.

By joining with others to perform analysis and going together as a team to talk about what you've found, you are creating a stronger case for the conclusions you've come to and you're demonstrating an understanding for the important players and experiential knowledge in the organization relating to your policy dilemma.

Coalition building, then, is about creating allies and engineering opportunities for those allies to inform your work. In other words, it is about being thorough and being collaborative — finding others to strengthen your knowledge gaps and helping fill knowledge gaps for others.

Being open to other forms of knowledge outside of the data analysis and being willing to challenge the validity of the data based on other information are two great places to start with this effort.

Finally, try to see your work as a service and to make that service available liberally across your organization. If you don't find yourself getting requests from some parts of your organization — reach out to them and start a conversation to find out what they need and how you might help. This will build your reputation in the organization, assemble an array of allies you can draw on to assist you when you need data for an analysis, and neutralize potential veto players.

Plus it's fun — you like data, right? Did you know people will often just give it to you if you ask?

5.4.4   Reputation Management

Data analysis is a craft — a craft you have to hone through experience and time. Unfortunately, it's also a craft where the difference between a shoddy job and an excellent job can be hard for non-analysts (and even other analysts) to see. This makes it all the harder sometimes, under time pressure, to do the work to the quality we need when we know that most of the hard work that ensures a quality result will go unseen.

Please resist this urge to whip through things. Others are trusting and relying on you.

Data are humbling. Data analysis is filled with traps you can fall into that lead you to get the wrong number or draw the wrong conclusion. Test your code. Understand your metadata. Document what you've done. Communicate clearly. You have to get the font right or you might lose a key veto player in a presentation. You have to use the right term to describe the standardized test error calculation, or you might look like you are unprepared. And, above all, you have to earn a reputation of fairness, accuracy, and integrity that your organization can rely on time and time again. This doesn't happen overnight. Be patient with yourself and give yourself the time, care, and attention that you need to hone your skills, practice your craft, get feedback you need to become the most extraordinary asset to the institution that you can be.

5.4.5 Timing

Being able to recognize when a policy window is open and when it is closed is an important skill. If a request for analysis is happening in a policy window, it is time to "suit up" and give it your best shot under a short deadline. The approximate answer in a policy window is better than the most precise answer five days later. Knowing this allows you to be strategic about where you spend your time and where you spend your effort. It also helps you safeguard your reputation (as discussed above) by adding the appropriate caveats to your work and not biting off more than you can chew.

When you are not in a policy window, it is a good time to be preparing for the next one. Automating your data cleaning, building your metadata, learning about new data collections that can be useful, and building relationships with new areas in your organization are all great ways to "train" for the times the windows are open.

Each of these investments will give you the scaffolding you need to give timely and accurate information when the time comes. It can also be a great way to help keep up the pressure needed to open policy windows — by providing those working in policy areas with a steady stream of information they can use to make their case.

In our experience policy windows are brief and often unpredictable. The best way to prepare is to learn how to recognize them, and to build infrastructure that you can take advantage of when they open up.

---○---

5.5   Conclusion

Thanks for sticking with this chapter. Just the word "politics" can leave many folks disinterested or disenchanted, so we appreciate you reading what we have to offer here to try to help you make your way in the halls of the hierarchy.

Here is where we leave you, dear reader. Your skills as a data analyst mean you have great power to influence policy decisions in your organization and beyond. Policymakers are hungry for information, and you are a prime source of what they need to do their work. This power comes with responsibility — a responsibility to understand the political process, understand the way information will be used, and a commitment to deliver the most accurate information you can. That's why you took this job, right?

CHAPTER 6

Moments of Truth: The Importance of Descriptive Statistics

6.1 Introduction

Descriptive statistics[1] (or "descriptives") tell you about your dataset by **describing** basic patterns in the data. They don't test hypotheses or predict outcomes. They are the more straightforward cross-tabulations (or "crosstabs") of frequencies and means, the single-variable distribution graphs (such as histograms), and the simple bar graphs of the data analyst's toolkit.

In most research, descriptives are primarily used to display the patterns in analytic findings. We believe they should also be recognized for the critical check they can provide on analytic assumptions – both yours and those of others. What is more, they help make your work digestible so your analysis can reach lay audiences in an accessible way; that is, without scaring or alienating folks who might not have a strong mathematical background. They also help build your intuition for a dataset as an analyst—to help give you a sense of the weight and scale of the data and what values are normal and which are abnormal—which is useful in all future work with a dataset.

To these ends, the following pages make the case for using solid descriptive statistics to generate valuable insights during your in-house research and in partnership with others. We think this

---

[1] http://daynebatten.com/2016/06/counting-hard-data-science/

discussion is worth having, because descriptives often get over-looked as the key tools they actually are due to their simplicity.

In our collective opinion this is giving them short shrift, especially in the administrative data analysis context, so we decided this chapter was an important one to write. Ultimately, descriptives tell us what the data say in and of themselves, and we think these can be some of the most powerful stories that you ever tell through your work.

Below, we'll share insights from our DATACOPE forum discussions on conducting in-house descriptive analytics and we'll outline how you can use them to help external researchers meet a higher bar for appropriate, rigorous inquiries—from the initial research requests, to vetting the findings themselves.

We'll share some strategies we've found successful as well as some cautionary tales about testable data assumptions—with huge implications—that nevertheless often go untested. We'll offer suggestions for avoiding situations like those, and, assuming we've made a sufficient case for you to integrate these checks into your daily practices, we provide some short, time-saving lines of code for the most common checks in Chapter 7.

If you're looking for a discussion of more advanced methodologies, a chapter in the next volume will cover inferential correlational and causal models (e.g., regressions). You'll find that we think descriptives have a foundational role there too, because if you use them well, they can replace model assumptions with empirical data. For instance, descriptives help test identification strategy assumptions about observable variables[2] ("observables") sufficiently controlling for selection on latent[3] or unobservable variables (called "unobservables" by econometricians). This is especially relevant now under the new Every Student Succeeds Act (ESSA) Tier IV or Promising Evidence allowance for correlational studies with selection controls[4].

---

[2] https://en.wikipedia.org/wiki/Observable_variable

[3] https://en.wikipedia.org/wiki/Latent_variable

[4] https://www2.ed.gov/policy/elsec/leg/essa/guidanceuseseinvestment.pdf

For this volume though, we'll focus exclusively on how descriptive methods shed light on the observable data itself in order to inform its appropriate role in any intended analysis. To that end, we align this material with the context of the other chapters here on data management, most specifically Chapter 2 on metadata and Chapter 4 on data requests. Hopefully you'll appreciate the method to our madness along the way!

6.2 Why write this chapter?

6.2.1 Because the data's origin story matters.

In any environment, doing sound analysis means knowing what you're working with. As in, really, really knowing it. This is why checking your assumptions before diving in is so key and why good analysis and good administrative data management go hand in hand. But while we've come by necessity to see those roles as inseparable, this is not how most of us were trained to do analysis. Before launching into specific techniques in Chapter 7, we'll try to help you quickly embrace and adopt the practice in your work—hopefully sparing you from having to learn the hard way.

Administrative data management ideally encompasses all the stages from raw data collection to data preparation for use. Yet these stages are often split across the IT-oriented and analysis-oriented domains, without a standard data prep continuum. This can make a full understanding of the data less tractable, even with good systems in place at each stage of the data pipeline.

In this way, administrative data differs fundamentally from the survey data most of us empirical researchers were trained to use. In surveys, a standardized system of pre-established statistical checks and documentation are used throughout each stage—from design and collection, to preparation and use. Decisions about which subpopulations will be oversampled and by how much are thoroughly documented, as are the mechanisms by which and the number of times each participant will be prompted to answer each question and the exact values the surveyors record for non-responses and values outside of a range (like top-coded incomes)[5].

In theory, similar controls and documentation can be designed and built for administrative data collection processes, but in practice, there are often just too many different sources and stages with different business rules that also keep changing over time to make this wieldy (see our discussion of the Holy Grail in Chapter 2).

It's necessary to regularly check-in with your data directly—in addition to your metadata (again, think the Round Table and the Grail). This is particularly true in the data analysis stage, which often draws on a wide range of the data elements from different administrative areas. Analysis may include cohorts reaching back to your legacy system—so even good metadata of your current business rules won't be enough to guide the analyst.

In this chapter and the next we share descriptives from public resources we created for a state with a national, university-based research center that fulfilled academic researcher data requests on behalf of the SEA.[6] Check out this metadata graphic in Figure 6.1 created to help researchers quickly grasp the potential and limitations of the broader linked administrative data files beyond the commonly used test records. Before producing potential policy inferences with this state's data, researchers can gauge whether their proposed longitudinal analysis can be supported or not and for which cohorts.

This is certainly blunt metadata still. In the figures beyond this one we show the kind of descriptive statistics needed to shed light on the specific data collection quirks in each content area and time period. A good example of this is the "exit type" variable for determining whether each student was promoted or retained;

---

[5] https://en.wikipedia.org/wiki/Top-coded

[6] North Carolina's Department of Public Instruction (NC DPI) has an arrangement with Duke University to process researcher requests for their archive of records housed there.

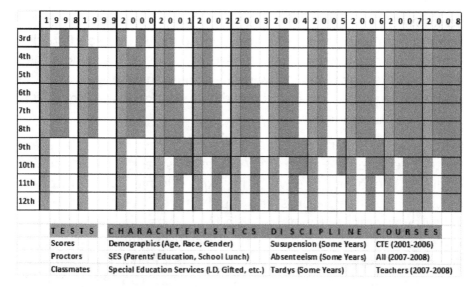

FIGURE 6.1: State legacy system of linked administrative records by grade and year.

transferred to another school, district, or state; dropped out; or graduated under various definitions (etc., etc.) at the end of each year. These are variables tracking detailed definitions determined by policies varying constantly over time. Was the change in your data that year the introduction of a new diploma type in your state or just a code change? This is an important question to ask before saying something about a shift in graduation rates, for example.

The bottom line is that administrative data processes are harder to keep track of than survey designs in the research environment generally are, but the necessity of knowing—with as much accuracy as possible—what the data do and do not represent is still a very important thing to keep in mind.

The more aware you are of how your data came to be, the better your ability to critique the various assumptions required before developing your analysis or helping others carry out their work. For instance, is it okay to do that slick math you're going to try to do on the data you've selected to work with, or do characteristics of the data preclude you from doing that math since it's not going to allow you to make valid inferences?

To know whether you are successfully representing things like student inputs and outcomes, you need to have a deep and precise understanding of where those measures came from and how they were collected, as well as how those collections change over time and what that tells you about the data's strengths and limitations for different purposes.

Recall the increasing coverage of student data files in the state system depicted in Figure 6.1. Among those additional data files added in the later years were the exit code files we mentioned, as well as course records and much more. These were important developments for being able to analyze high school years, since the commonly used test records covered only 3rd-8th grade completely. Researchers conducting dropout analysis, wanted to compare cohorts over time, and there were too few years still of exit data. They saw student test record frequencies holding through what they thought were pre-dropout grades of 9th and 10th, and then falling before graduation, and decided the sample appeared essentially intact and representative. But this graph in Figure 6.2 of student records in all administrative files (in red) relative to (blue) test files only, showed how many high school students would be missing from their analysis. And a safe guess you could make is that those students not testing in Physics and Algebra II in high school are not a random subset when it comes to the propensity to drop out.

Here are some questions along these lines we've found helpful to ask before we dive in are things like:

- Which program areas have data on all relevant students, and how representative are the subsets for the others?
- Were the outcomes you're comparing before and after a policy change consistently measured over that time period?
- Did a measure change over the time period you're looking at (e.g. did a scale change on an assessment? Did the assessment itself change, etc.?)
- Do time-invariant variables such as birthdate or race vary over time in your data, when they shouldn't? (Though, the notion of

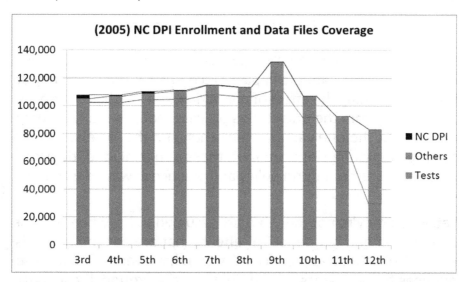

FIGURE 6.2: Graph confirms what assumptions about high school test records miss.

time-invariant gender records seems somewhat archaic to us now.)

To find all this out, you need good data management and good metadata. It is also important to recognize the answers may not all be in the data themselves - you may have to ask others or show them descriptives as a way to get their feedback and draw out their expertise in solving a problem - we call this using descriptives to build expertise on-ramps.

You also need to look at your data at each stage of your work and from many angles to really know which tests it can support and which questions it can answer. Think of this work, using descriptives to help you know your data really well at all times, like stick-handling in hockey. Whether you're skating towards the net to shoot, pass the puck, receive a pass, or intercept one, it is the one essential skill you constantly apply no matter what you or others are going to need to do at any moment.

6.2.2   Because modeling is better with fewer guesses

In the applied arena, complex models may be used to make policy inferences or evaluate the impact of a particular practice. They do this by estimating the effect of one variable on another, controlling for all else. From the outset, this process requires many assumptions about the one variable, the other, and the "all else." When the model assumptions are met, these sophisticated identification strategies can inform policy and practice in ways descriptives cannot.

Yet, when they're not met—but are assumed to have been—these models can find "evidence" of effects that are not there or "disprove" truly effective practices. This can have very serious consequences for educators and students on the ground. It can mean laws (not) getting made and/or funding (not) getting allocated to one program or another.

In our experience, the primacy given to understanding the math undergirding statistical principles applied to the data can sometimes eclipse the need to determine whether it's even appropriate to apply that math to the underlying data in the first place. For example, a study of the effects of chronic absenteeism or class size reduction needs to first make sure it is measuring absenteeism or class size correctly, in addition to appropriately modeling the effects as, say, nonlinear.

Descriptives can help empirically ensure both, and while they might not be all that "flashy" in the world of modeling—when done well, they can be some of the most potent and useful work that you do.

Yet, how many of us, in a push to respond to a request for analysis from our leadership, have skipped right over testing key assumptions about a dataset before running the tests we're asked for? Not including that step could prevent you from catching something like a non-response[7] bias in what you think is supposed to be the full population dataset.

---

[7] https://en.wikipedia.org/wiki/Participation_bias

For instance, what if career-technical course data were only re-ported for students reaching a concentration level of credits, and not all students taking the courses? Or for students without test scores, especially students with disabilities, who are then dropped from some key datasets? Not examining the data set descriptively first to surface these limitations could lead you to erroneously think that something you observe in your analysis is generalizable to the population when it really might not be.

Further, with the development of longitudinal administrative data systems, analysts can conduct strong descriptive work much more readily than before. It is because of these systems, which strive to integrate data from formerly disparate collections across the universe or population of students and teachers every year, that analysts can now replace many of the critical assumptions and unobservables that much statistical work has relied upon with descriptive checks and observables.

Instead of assuming a subset is representative of your data and normal, homoscedastic[8], balanced, or otherwise, you can actually test these conditions and use empirical facts about the datasets themselves to inform your next steps. That means the promise of fewer guesses and more terra firma empiricism to build your work upon.

While not a panacea, such systems create an extraordinary op-portunity for analysis. If you've got good data management and metadata stewardship happening in your institution, and you in-corporate descriptive statistical analysis as a foundational step in any work you do, you are empowered to do fundamentally better science. Additionally, as the person likely responsible for the data external researchers use, you're able to inform and improve theirs as well.

Because the risks (and rewards) are so high in this environment, tight data management, attentiveness to the metadata, and taking the time to explore the dataset with descriptive analysis before working with it in more complex ways are all crucial steps in the

---

[8] https://en.wikipedia.org/wiki/Homoscedasticity

process of doing the kind of work that can shape our social institutions.

We think that's a big deal and worth committing to.

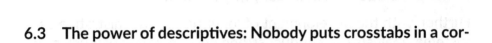

6.3   The power of descriptives: Nobody puts crosstabs in a corner

While descriptives won't by themselves be able to answer the why questions, these multidimensional depictions of the data can speak to the **who, what, where, and when** questions you'll likely need to answer in a wide range of your work.

For instance, decision-makers may be working from incorrect assumptions about the number and type of students covered under different programs. You may have information on the number of students in each subgroup, class, grade, school, and year right at your fingertips. You could provide much-needed insight so that key choices are based on data and not anecdotes.

This is some of the pivotal work that you'll do as an analyst, so while you may not find counts of students or teachers by demographic group and participation in a particular activity or program terribly groundbreaking, they constitute some of the essential information you can provide in many contexts. They also represent foundational, testable data that must undergird the assumptions required of any more complex model being run on those data; in-house or by external researchers as we've covered above.

That a crosstab could be so critical may come as somewhat of a shocker. It's been our observation that the convention in academic research is not necessarily to take an iterative approach to using the data, which is completely opposite to how this unfolds in the applied context.

In academia sometimes those running regressions and generating tables are not even the same people. In well-resourced academic environments, researchers might task research assistants with producing the critical descriptive tables, while they themselves are often independently generating their hypotheses and selecting the appropriate statistical methodologies for testing those hypotheses.

In the applied setting, work is generally conducted in a collaborative way. (Checking one another's work during code review, anyone? Review processes before posting products to your institution's website, anybody? etc.) And the standard for your work is probably geared towards making your products as accessible and non-technical as possible so the materials can be disseminated widely and efficiently.

In our experience, the divergent approach to working with the data is a mistake and we take issue with the low priority that summary statistics tables of the underlying data are given across a lot of academic work. Sometimes, they're only even included in appendices. They are generally referenced to support the major decisions that went into paring down the full data to the analytic set used in the model, with reassurances that some aspect of the samples can be seen in the tables to vary only in trivial ways. But it is often clear that those tables and the information they contain did not play a big part in the study designs.

For example, more than one published education study has cited a small difference in mean test scores between the full and analytic sample as confirmation their subset is representative, and then touted their model effects of the same magnitude as a policy-relevant difference in outcomes. Others have staked their findings of successful school practices on having sufficiently controlled for student household income differences, while the appendix frequency tables show the Free/Reduced Lunch (FRL) eligibility values missing for critical years and grades.

These kinds of oversights can easily be avoided if descriptives are given the attention they deserve and are used to inform the next steps in the work the way that they should. Honestly, would you treat your single greatest means of understanding the data like that? That'd be like a member of your awayteam[9] forgetting their tricorder. Tsk tsk. Who picked the new guy to come along?

Think of it this way, we often talk about decisions being "data driven," in terms of policies and practices being based on evidence gleaned from complex models. But, a critical thing for us to remember as analysts, is that we need to be much more data driven about the decisions that go into how we build such models in the first place.

To that end, we think it's much better to be conscientious about the characteristics of the data at the design stage than to have to call into question the results of a given study after the fact (by taking a look at what the descriptives actually said in the first place before you or someone else did all that work).

Get your ingredients in order before you think you're going to try to bake. You can't just substitute baking soda straight up for baking powder. Unless you're aiming for really, really tall cookies!

We'll try to resist hammering this point throughout the rest of the chapter and the next, and just ask you to try to keep it in the front of your mind... always.

6.4   Describing your data early and often

To leverage descriptives in your daily work, and to maybe even develop some standard checks that you incorporate into all your output, we'll unpack the three stages of data prep and analysis where these are most helpful and highlight some best practices.

This section is geared toward helping you jump in and implement these recommendations by providing some guidance for best practices in incorporating these kinds of descriptives into your workflow. We're highlighting valuable lessons from our experience with

---

[9] https://en.wikipedia.org/wiki/Away_team_(Star_Trek_term)

descriptives in data prep and analysis under the different headings listed below.

At every point in the progression, from raw data to a final prepped analytic dataset, necessary changes are made to the data that need a close eye kept on them to be sure they don't change something fundamental to any inferences. We think of there being three different datasets or stages to consider for data decisions going into each model, and we'll describe these in turn below.

6.4.0.1 Data Stage 1: Raw data files

The initial raw data is very different from what the analyst will ultimately be working with. Not the least of which, because some of these files can contain the personal identifiers. These initial data files can be in various states of rawness, however. They could be "as reported" by the field or they could be "cleaned and verified" by the field, but still personally identifiable. A more granular discussion of these data decisions and their documentation are provided in Chapter 3 on IT, Chapter 2 on metadata, and Chapter 4 on data requests.

6.4.0.2 Data Stage 2: Prepped datasets (or cut data files)

These interim manifestations of the data are the linked, cleaned, de-identified data files that you prepare for in-house use and for external researchers as described in Chapter 4. Some of the inherent data decisions were also described in that chapter. Here, these are the datasets that you would perform the descriptive analyses on to get started in your work.

Specifically, this is the stage of the data analysis prep to document—for yourself, your audiences, and the researchers. It should include details like what you know about the students, etc., as represented in this first, fullest administrative data sample of the universe or population. (Remember, this can be the universe of students, but it can also be the universe of schools, teachers, classes, tests, etc.) Every decision after this snapshot of the universe will alter the perspective of it, and this version should be documented to compare and check assumptions about potential biases. The most obvious instance of this is when you are creating an analytic subset of the population. This can be necessary for a number of reasons: it could be due to the specific focus of the analysis (e.g., only students with disabilities) or the structure of the cohorts (e.g., excluding retained students and transfers). Summary statistics of the initial full dataset, relative to the analytic sets, are essential.

In the previous figures, we showed the limitations descriptives revealed about the student record coverage for content and grades outside of the core 3rd-8th math and reading test score files. The state where we created these public resources were one of the first to provide access to test score data with links to teachers. As you can imagine, dozens of high-profile teacher value-added studies were published with these data. Unfortunately, the robust teacher and student test files were connected through the weak link of the test proctor record. Course records, which came out much later, were needed for true teacher matching. But even after these records were available, researchers kept working with the more straightforward proctor linked test files. The histograms in 6.3 show the volume of teachers and students omitted from these "statewide" value-added analyses. In just this one cross-section and grade, you can see the darker shade of proctor matches relative to the 95% of 4th grade students matched to teachers through course records. Then multiply that by all the grades and cohorts strung together in these longitudinal studies.

In addition to limiting the data to subsamples, analysis may also require aggregating up from more granular observations in the initial data to form a simpler dataset to work with. You will want to document the business rules for collapsing this additional information into, say, single student-year values, and provide some description of the true initial variation. For example, if students are allowed to retest in some key subjects but you're cutting an analytic dataset of exactly one observation per student-year, you should provide information on the retesting variation that will otherwise be lost, but may be very important, to the analyst. You'll

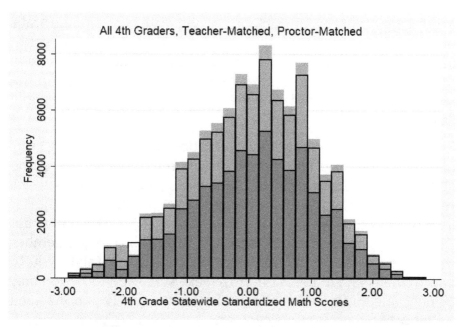

FIGURE 6.3: Commonly used test files needed course records to match teachers.

want to clarify your aggregation decision: did you take the mean of the two tests, just the last, or just the first? And you'll want to provide some description of the retest take-up rate, maybe by subgroup or initial score, and maybe the magnitude and range of the score changes between tests. The analyst will need to know if there were widespread retesting in certain high-stake grades or subjects, if that resulted in big improvements in scores, and if it occurred more among students in some schools, districts, or demographic groups than others.

The same recommendations apply to students changing schools within the year. How many school moves were there; how long were they in the school they tested in? Educators have told us how important it is in designing supplemental instruction plans to distinguish between low-scoring in-coming students who struggled with the same material over time, and those who were exposed to different material across schools. Other data that need describing in this way are the higher than annual frequency collections, such as monthly suspension and absenteeism data. (In one state, providing these additional descriptions helped researchers studying outside influences affecting student behavior to understand that they needed to account for strong seasonal patterns in the suspension data—surprise... kids act out more just before school calendar breaks.)

Finally, these steps of paring observations and aggregating granular data, may be undertaken by the external researcher in the stage we describe next. If that's the case, you will want to stress that they describe their transformations of the data along similar lines. Note: we're saying that "the analyst will need to know," but that doesn't mean they'll think to ask the data directly. Remember, that's not how we've all been trained. It will likely fall to you to inform them, and it doesn't hurt to make sure they know you may be checking this same variation in-house as well. (They don't need to know how insanely busy you are...)

6.4.0.3   Data Stage 3: Analytic dataset(s)

From the researcher's perspective (or more likely, the research assistant's), this is where the data prep begins. The de-identified data files you prepped for them are considered their raw data, and they will start to cull and combine these in ways that will likely result in analytic samples representing something very different than the universe you entrusted them with. We say "entrusted" here because these data and the work that will come from them are about some of the most important people and institutions in our society; children and schools. There are also pretty stringent data privacy laws[10] at the federal and state levels. They're stringent for a reason and we think everyone should remember that all the time. (Ok, we'll get off our soapbox now.)

As the researchers are making decisions about which records to retain and which to drop from their analysis dataset, you will want them to also be able to account for how they have altered the set you've provided to them and to demonstrate the types

---

[10] https://studentprivacy.ed.gov/

and degree of resulting biases that may enter their analyses. This simple bar graph in 6.4 is included in the appendix of a paper that studied statewide dropout determinants for a 3rd grade cohort.[11] It was included, in addition to some attrition analysis, to describe clearly for readers the sample attrition involved with this kind of longitudinal span.

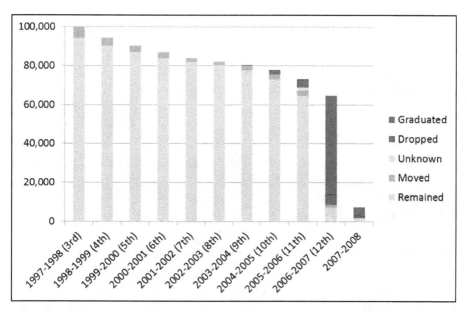

FIGURE 6.4: Analytic output should be transparent about sample cohort attrition.

The same is true for analytic variable constructions. For instance, is their constructed variable for economically disadvantaged students a time-varying variable that may not count low-income students at higher grades, when they are less likely to be identified as such, and if so, what are the identification attrition rates from that subgroup?

Also, a quick note here to be clear about the bias we're talking about in this section so we all stay on the same page. Generally, when researchers discuss potential biases in their analysis, they are

---

[11]For links to this and other papers these examples are drawn from, see DJ's bio.

referring to their models, or identification strategies, like whether they can assume they have controlled for class assignment biases in teacher value-added models by including previous grade test scores. But for our purposes here, we are talking about the potential bias introduced into the model by altering the data in order to analyze it—by any specification.

This is where the descriptive statistics really shine, because they can help you help your (or the researchers') analysis. They help you make data-driven decisions about what you're going to do (or researchers are going to do) with the data. (Otherwise, seriously... really tall cookies... like taller than they are wide.)

———————————⬡———————————

6.5   Three handy rules for leveraging descriptives

Fundamentally, many of the common and critical data decisions are made prior to most studies' descriptive analyses, when researchers or research assistants are determining which records to bring into the main analyses and are expecting their values to arrive unscathed. The mechanics of these decisions are important and we hope we've provided you with a sense of why you should pay careful, close attention to analytic dataset prep decisions as well as work attentive descriptive analysis into your standard operating procedures before you run with more complex work.

One of Us (Wendy)

And here's what that can look like. When Vermont passed its Universal Pre-K law, Wendy and her team designed a path analysis to investigate the relationships between particular types of pre-k program delivery and student outcomes in pre-k assessments, kindergarten readiness assessments, and then later in a third-grade assessment. Based on advisement from the various data stewards from both the education and human services agencies that co-administer the universal pre-k system, this methodologically seemed the most appropriate approach to answer the questions that all the various stakeholders had. And it seemed reasonable to assume the data would be available to support that type of analysis.

Unfortunately, as is often the case in the world of administrative data (especially when more than one organization and its data are involved), there proved to be too much missingness once the many different data sets were finally matched up to create the analysis sample for the planned analysis. It just couldn't support the planned work due to very unequal and non-random distribution of missingness being so pronounced.

Instead of trying to run the model anyways in zealous pursuit of the more complex questions (Wendy does have a tendency to get a little excited sometimes), the team fell back on leveraging descriptives to ensure that the analysis would be methodologically sound and appropriate for the data that were available and the high stakes of the work.

In the end, the most sophisticated statistical test the team got to run was a chi square to note that the analysis sample was not statistically different from the entire state population of pre-k students; but when the more targeted questions about program type, geographic location, etc., were included, representativeness fell apart. Hence, no model.

There's a pretty big silver lining though. The descriptives were insightful in their own right and continue to be some of the most important data available for discussion. This was also such an instructive process of discovery about the strengths and limitations of the different data collections that many targeted efforts at improving data quality were able to be launched. These efforts are paying off as the quality among these collections is improving and the prospects of running more complex analyses are on the horizon in the coming years.

The point of sharing this example is that because this type of work can have such a deep and profound impact on the lived experience around you (laws can get made or unmade, programs can be funded or not, etc.), our standards have to be extremely high before we try to use the data in the ways we plan to. The reality is that they often can't support the lofty designs we may have without much careful, dedicated stewardship. That can take a lot of time. Years even. (Wendy increased her shoe budget when she learned this. It's her way of coping).

From the maintenance of multiple alias tables for variations of first, middle, and last names to increase matching rates, to thoughtful application of screening tests for outliers or anomalies in the data (e.g., did an historically diverse organization accidentally report a very homogeneous student population by mistake?), to checking a set for non-random missingness before trying to use it, all of these practices add up to the kind of science that can hold water. The next section expands on this topic a bit more with some general rules we've found helpful in these efforts.

6.5.0.1   Data Prep Rule 1: Check for bias before running analysis

There's a saying among tradespeople that "a good paint job is 90% prep." The same is true for good analysis. It is very possible for decisions made at the data prep stage we're talking about here to introduce more bias than incorrect model assumptions alone. Yet, unlike the model assumptions, these data assumptions aren't often tested for bias in the course of the analysis. As the person whose office or cubicle everyone eventually finds when anyone anywhere reports results with your data, you'll have to account for those results even if the problems were generated by the external researchers who've already completely moved on. (Note: some of the most high-profile data errors are made by others analyzing federal aggregate data collected on your schools in your state or district, which could have been prevented using the same descriptive steps.)

You can imagine how data pitfalls that are easy to miss in-house become even harder to catch as the data transfer to the researchers. Sometimes these decisions could render the analysis extremely misleading. They can attribute meaning to a relationship found in the analysis that is actually due to the criteria used to drop records in the prep stage. This glossing over of the true data implications is why it is essential that you try to persuade external researchers to confirm these decisions with you before moving on to publish the work somewhere.

If possible, try to cultivate the relationship so that you can go over any red flags with them together before publication. If this doesn't happen, you might otherwise be left to try to repair the damage after the fact—an ounce of prevention being worth a pound of cure, or closing barn doors after horses have bolted, etc. Sickness, lost horses, and cleaning up after problematic analysis; three things not high on anyone's wish list.

6.5.0.2 Data Prep Rule 2: Run the descriptives yourself

Ultimately, one way you'll be prepared to recognize important potential errors and provide some evidence to the researchers to get them to address those potential issues is if you have explored and documented the full dataset in advance.

This would be an extra step to work into the data request process, where you document what you're sending, or through regular documentation practices of descriptives you run as part of your in-house analyses. Some examples of this are: before and after descriptive checks for merges and aggregations, and variable distribution checks. We recommend you work these kinds of explorations into your own analysis efforts so that you not only know the data well before you need to help others work with it, but that you also are able to highlight areas where data quality could be improved. Note: external researchers will often confuse their misreading of your administrative data with quality issues with the raw data–descriptives help you and them better understand both potential sources of trouble.

6.5.0.3 Data Prep Rule 3: Share what you learn

Every time you and your team or your external researchers run descriptives, you learn something more about the underlying data and the populations and context they represent. The simple descriptive tools we provide shortcuts for in the Chapter 7 are designed to generate simple outputs as well. Try to get into the habit of taking snapshots of this output and compiling those as resources to be drawn on for your team and others to learn from. The most time-consuming thing about tables and graphs is the formatted production of these for reports and publication—you don't need all that formatting for the purpose of a resource. Just make sure it's clear what all variable labels refer to and what observations are and are not included, what years of the data the run was done on, etc.

You can save yourself and others a lot of time and trouble, and avoid invalid findings, by keeping a running tab on data quality issues that you've discovered. For instance, if your descriptive analysis, or that of a researcher's, found a data hole of sorts in a given program or school or district in a given year... best not to keep that to yourself.

And even beyond data quality issues, you may have some sensitivity analysis findings from your descriptive snapshots to arm your analytic staff and researchers with. For instance, maybe you've documented attrition rates in FRL eligibility status as students in higher grades stop identifying or participating. Or maybe you succeeded in getting a previous researcher to conduct and share those descriptives. Either way, you can now pass those along with the next relevant data request. Learning more about the data can reveal potential as well, not just limitations. (Those monthly suspension plots we referenced earlier taught us something about student needs as well as our model's need to adjust for seasonal effects.)

To help reduce the burden for these kinds of tasks, we remind you again that we cover some best practices for how you can approach the data request process more fully in Chapter 4 and how metadata can help avoid reinvented wheels in Chapter 2, as well as the batch codes for streamlining descriptive practices in-house in Chapter 7.

6.6   Words can't describe...

But tables and graphs can. So we are going to stop talking at you about the need for and role of descriptives, and let you get on to making use of the tools we share next.

As a final note, we just want to say that we know your job is already intensive with a lot of demands made on you. And we you know you obviously care about making a difference and know what's at stake... because you chose to work in this sector. We also understand that you wouldn't have this job if you didn't already have a strong command of the kinds of techniques we're talking about and their usefulness. Essentially, we know your data's in good hands!

To support you in your work, we wanted to be sure to make the strongest case we could for these tools, and help you make the strongest case to others... as you will need to. Because one casual data decision can completely invalidate the policy recommendations of a study and no model diagnostic will catch that. Every lost nuance in the data along the way means a potentially important insight into some aspect of learning or teaching or supporting both may get lost as well. There are textbooks full of methods discussions for running sharp or fuzzy regression discontinuities and maximum likelihood estimations of mixed-level models with modified random effects—but try finding one, outside of this chapter, with concrete steps for qualifying all important data decisions going into any of those analyses. We've learned in our own work, and through sharing strategies and horror stories with our DATA-COPE peers and others, how insistent you need to be in flipping the script and ensuring that the data itself is understood and respected as the powerful driver it is in any analysis.

We want to leave you with one more illustration we hope will inspire you. A pair of statewide research papers were originally based around some very slick panel data techniques analyzing 12 million student-year observations and hundreds of variables.[12] But, in presentations of the preliminary findings, practitioners kept intimating that the regressions could be foregone since everyone would just care about the information in this simple graph, Figure 6.5.

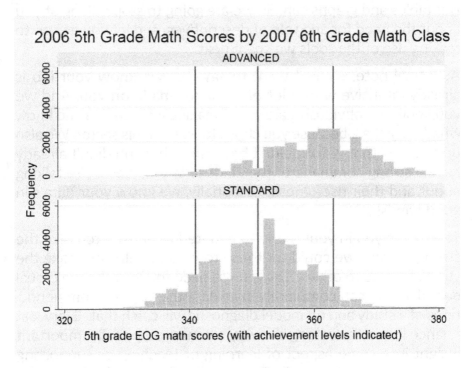

FIGURE 6.5: THE graph.

They were right. Nothing else in the analysis was found to be as informative as just this simple breakdown of 5th grade math scores leading to 6th grade advanced course assignments substantially overlapping with those of schoolmates who were not

---

[12]For the full paper see the link to DJ's work in her bio.

assigned. Simple. But it challenged study inferences that were based on common assumptions: that classes are not broken out systematically until they are observed in the data as Algebra I, and that assignments to more advanced courses are presumably based on previous test scores, since the assigned student group had a higher mean score. Looking at the data descriptively produces some of the most boring looking graphs you'll ever do, but it can change everything.

CHAPTER 7

Applying Tools of the Trade: Descriptive Data Commands in Context

---◇---

7.1 Introduction

In Chapter 6, we made a strong case for the essential role of descriptives in your work. Fundamentally, whether you're trying to use structural equation modeling[1] or crosstabs[2], the practices we described there for examining the appropriateness of an approach as well as documenting data decisions made throughout the work all apply. The more complex statistical regression models, whether run in-house or by external researchers, need to be based on assumptions about the data that are empirically defensible and preferably solid. Doing descriptives well helps you make sure you've done that groundwork and your foundations are firm.

This is integral to doing responsible data work in this arena because the more statistical adjustments a model makes, the more assumptions it makes and the more data decisions are required. This is especially so when these decisions are made externally and the inferences are high stakes. In cases like these, which you're likely to experience in the applied environment, you want to be able to implement practices that will add layers of transparency and checks to the work. Here, we get into the specific techniques you can use to do this.

In this chapter, we break out the data components into three

---

[1]https://en.wikipedia.org/wiki/Structural_equation_modeling

[2]https://en.wikipedia.org/wiki/Contingency_table

focus areas—the variables, values, and observations—and provide sample lines of statistical software code for working with them. But first, we look at the two broad types of descriptive techniques. Table 7.1 summarizes each of these breakdowns.

TABLE 7.1: Categories of descriptive tools and data components

Type of Descriptives	Descriptors	Summary statistics
	Depictors	Graphs of distributions and relationships (histograms, bar graphs)
Data Components	Variables	String, categorical, binary, constructed, etc.
	Values	Numbers, text, error flags, missings, etc.
	Observations	Student, teacher, student-year-subject, etc.

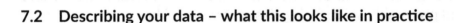

7.2   Describing your data – what this looks like in practice

We describe here the two broad types of the various descriptives you've got at your disposal. Then, following our discussion of the three data components, we share some simple time-saving lines of code for systematically using each type of descriptive to explore the different components.

7.2.1   Two types of descriptives

There are two main types of these descriptive tools:[3]

1.   the summary statistics tables that **describe** your data, and

---

[3]In other places these are referred to as numerical and graphical exploratory data analysis, or EDA.

2.   the single- and multiple-variable graphs that **depict** it.

7.2.1.1   Summary statistics: Descriptions of data

Summary statistics are generally the first and second statistical moments[4] of the means and the variance of the continuous variables (along with the minimum and maximum values) and the counts or frequencies of the discrete variables.

These are generally viewed for the entire sample as well as broken out across different categories (such as by year, district, grade level, student subgroup, etc.,) when first familiarizing oneself with a new dataset and often again at the findings stage. However, we recommend running these subgroup tabulations throughout all stages. Important insights about potential outliers and missingness[5] come to the fore through examining summary statistics, and this information can be critical (remember non-response bias[6] analysis before you start your work, anyone?).

Statistical software command lines, shared further below, demonstrate efficient ways to view different combinations of discrete and continuous variables. We recommend you run commands like these throughout your data prep and analytic work, for instance, at every merge or paring of the data. Generating quick tables that combine the discrete categories with the means and other statistical moments for the continuous variables can be really illuminating and save you the hassle of running statistical tests that aren't appropriate or needed for a given the dataset. Whenever possible, always opt for saving time and energy, especially during legislative session...

---

[4] https://en.wikipedia.org/wiki/Moment_(mathematics)

[5] https://en.wikipedia.org/wiki/Missing_data

[6] https://en.wikipedia.org/wiki/Participation_bias

7.2.1.2   Graphs: Depictions of data

The same information about individual variables and related variables that you might use a summary table to describe could also be depicted in visuals like graphs or charts.

These are different uses of graphs than, say, the data visualizations[7] you may be doing for school accountability data reporting. For instance, you'll want to graph several variables together even if you are not presenting their relationships elsewhere, but you want to be informed about how they do or do not co-move to learn more about their reliability, variability, or confoundedness[8] (nobody likes a lurker - just saying).

For instance, if you are doing an analysis of class size effects, you will want to first explore the true range of class sizes and distribution of all students across them, as well as the distribution of different types of students across them. A widely-cited study claimed to show class size reduction were bad investments by analyzing effects after first "trimming" classes to only those with 10-25 students and dropping students in any instructional programs, under the assumption that they were taught in separate rooms. Don't do that. Instead, you can do a quick check of the landscape with a simple histogram. You can run one for each of the student types you need to know about (or overlay a local polynomial or other smoothed values line, as in Figure 7.1).

We provide some command lines and tips for using these visual tools to learn more about the underlying data. At this point, we also want to suggest that perhaps the highest-leverage visual tool for data exploration and prep is the one used less often for displaying results. These are variable distribution graphs[9] like the one in Figure 7.2. This is when you depict one continuous variable's distribution of values over your sample. Your sample could be a group or a population, depending on the collection mechanism

---

[7] https://nces.ed.gov/pubsearch/pubsinfo.asp?pubid=NFES2017016

[8] https://en.wikipedia.org/wiki/Confounding

[9] https://en.wikipedia.org/wiki/Frequency_distribution

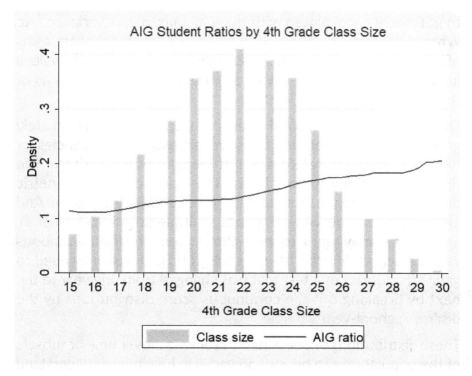

FIGURE 7.1: Simple histogram shows class size increasing with smoothed gifted-program ratio.

and requirements, and those details are things that should be known before you or others start your analysis.

For example, viewing the distribution of math or reading test scores over all 5th grade students should reveal a fairly normal distribution, with tails inside the scale score range. You may be assuming this form of the distribution is a given and only be in the habit of testing it if you thought something might be askew. We recommend that you check the distribution, and we also strongly recommend encouraging your external researchers to do the same.

It is also critical to view the distribution of other variables that we don't normally associate parametric distributions with, so that you can learn more of what you need to know about those data as well. This is especially true for any variables you construct for analysis, such as class sizes or school FRL student percentages, to get quickly acquainted with the min, max, mean, variance, etc. What is the expanse, are there outliers, are there secondary areas of concentration beyond the mean, how widespread are the values in each direction (i.e., how long are the tails)? And is any or all of this what you pictured?

Distributions can be viewed through histograms, which discretely group the shares of observations (by percentages, frequencies, or densities) across different levels of the continuous variable. The distributions can also be estimated by a host of non-parametric density estimation techniques like kernel density estimation. And either type can be viewed across multiple subsamples. For instance, you may want to view the dispersion of a continuous variable across different student subgroups. Or you may need to gauge the impact of a test that was changed from one year to the next by breaking out the continuous score distributions by the discrete school-year variable.

These distributions of one variable broken out over time or subsets of the population can be very powerful in helping you understand coverage, variation, representativeness, and whether or not you're going to violate assumptions before you start to try to run anything (remember: save time, save effort). Below, we provide examples and batch codes for a range of these approaches, but first we cover the three relevant data components.

7.2.2   Keeping it real (in the abstract data sense):

7.2.2.1   Data Component 1: Variables

There's a reason they're not called constants. What exactly each variable measures, how, and how well, needs to be examined in detail at every dataset prep stage—from raw to analytic. The variables and their values, can... you guessed it... vary a lot. But we want their variation to keep the true reflection of the information most accurately collected. Sometimes, the most accurate variation is at the raw data stage and can get distorted. Other times, the information becomes more accurate as the raw data is prepped. And all of this requires close inspection of the patterns in the data.

What varies within and across variables are the values (described next). But it is important to note that variable formats can also change between statistical software packages, causing lots of unexpected problems that descriptives can catch. For instance, many merge variables, like school codes, are inherently string values, not numeric, but they can get converted back and forth along the way. This can cause school codes to drop leading zeros—leading your merges to drop schools. In the sample statistical codes sections, we demonstrate descriptive commands for each of these variable types.

7.2.2.2 Data Component 2: Values

One of the biggest unintended variable changes that can occur involves the correct use of missing values vs. zeros. There are, roughly speaking, two types of missing values in administrative data.

The first, are the actual data points with no value that can be reported. These are the student-year-subject data points under the test score variable that register the character(s) that your business rules or your statistical program uses to code genuine missings (e.g., a space, a decimal, a negative number, the abbreviation N/A). These are true missing values, but still very important to describe the extent of, because any observations missing statistically essential information—in even one field—are omitted from regressions and other statistical procedures.

These omissions can introduce more potential bias—because missing values are also more frequent across certain subpopulations of students, such as highly mobile students, students with disabilities, economically disadvantaged students, and chronically absent or frequently suspended students. And it is not just complex statistical models. The same missing values cause even simple analytics, like subgroup means to be way off. But descriptives, like frequencies and means of other variables, can be run on the observations with missing values to compare them to the full sample. Descriptives can also help the analyst figure out the reason for the missing values in some cases. For example, Algebra I test scores will be missing for students in 8th grade who did not take the course, or took the course but not the test, or took the test but no score was recorded. These are important differences.

The other type of missing values are more inherently problematic. These are the ones that may be occurring inappropriately, such as the absence of a numerical value recorded when the actual value is zero. Similarly, zeros may be recorded when the actual value should be missing, either because the field was not applicable to that student or because the actual value for that student was unknown. Think of student absences or suspensions—if a student had none, there should be a zero, and if the number is unknown, there should be a missing value indicator—but the reality is that either can be misapplied.

These wrong values could be entered in the raw data, by the data entry person or the input field's default setting. Good systems clarify and/or force the exact values for N/A or skips, missing values or NULL, and actual zero values. But variables can still inadvertently switch between missings and zeros throughout the data prep stages as well. This can happen during merges and through aggregations. This is why you should run diagnostic descriptives of the frequencies and means of all the variables throughout all data prep stages.

It's important to realize that exactly because these types of changes are unintended, you won't necessarily know where to check—so by 'checking' we also mean 'scanning' for potential problems you may not have anticipated. The histograms are good descriptive tools for that, as are summary tables and single-variable tabulations.

Non-missing values can also change during the merging and aggregating steps throughout the analytic data prep. Collapsing observations or attributing group aggregates from different level data sources, such as aggregating individual student scores up to school means, can result in unintended values. You want to keep an eye on summary statistics to be sure that each merge or aggregation updated the values the way you intended. Did the calculation of the means include zeros as you intended, and did the ranking treat ties as you envisioned? Always, always, always... look at your data with every adjustment made... never assume it's transforming just exactly as you pictured it in your head.

7.2.2.3 Data Component 3: Observations

This point cannot be stressed enough. In general, analytic samples or subsets of administrative data files are not merely random subsets of the universe of data. Analytic datasets cull out individual observations that are deemed not to meet the objectives or requirements of the analysis. These alterations have consequences that should be acknowledged through a paper trail of descriptive evidence.

Data for students, for example, that do not fit into neat, complete, balanced packages or "intact cohorts" are often dropped in the analysis dataset prep steps in an effort to create a workable set to run the planned model. For example:

- An analysis may keep only students who progress through grades on-time for graduation, dropping all retained students.
- Often, only students with contiguous yearly observations are kept, which means any essential file with student data missing in one year drops the student altogether.
- Students who move between schools within the school year may be dropped.
- Small school populations in rural schools, charters, magnets, virtual schools, etc., can be dropped from analysis with school fixed or random effects (due to small Ns).

You are probably already starting to see the non-random patterns without even having to read the descriptive tables or see the graphs. For most students, being 'at-risk' is synonymous with grade retention, multiple school transfers, missing data points, etc.

On the whole, taking a look at the volume of data excluded from the final analysis dataset is an important step in determining the validity of the model or the potential bias introduced. This is the paper trail for how the researcher got from your several million student-year observations to the few hundred thousand they used in their regressions. That kind of attention to detail can also help you be aware that while the model may be unbiased on the average, it may be wildly inaccurate for small but important subsets of the data (e.g. remote students, students with disabilities, English Learners, etc.).

Also, remember, the initial full dataset to be prepped for analysis was itself likely constructed from several different data collections—covering different programs and assessments at different points in time. In order to analyze students, say, across many years, grades, and programs, these datasets needed to be made similar and merged. And every merge risks losing observations, for instance, because the collection frequencies vary or the key identifier (merging) variables may not match.

Some of the reduction in observations are practical decisions that should be described, such as consolidating within-year variation (of, say, school-year movers or re-testers.) But others, like the mis-merges, are mistakes that could be caught at the time by descriptives. Further below, we highlight the use of descriptives to track observations throughout the pairing and merging processes in more detail and provide some code.

To help you implement these recommendations, and all the others discussed above, this next part of the chapter demonstrates specific tools for implementing these kinds of descriptives into your work.

7.2.3   Command-relevant shorthand for data elements

7.2.3.1   Variables and their values

Using statistical programs, we talk about variables in terms of their stored values being string or numeric (or date). String variables use text values, even when they're numbers. Numeric variables that are categorical may be cardinal and use numbers to indicate categories, similar to string variables. (Ordinal categorical variables, such as Likert scales, are generally found in survey data.) When one of the categories is indicated as true, with a numeric value of 1, and false with a numeric value of 0, these are indicator or binary variables. (Note, these are still also technically categorical variables.) Finally, discrete variables (such as integers) have a countable number of values between any two values, whereas continuous variables have an infinite set.

TABLE 7.2: Numeric variable types

Name	Type	Example
varind	indicator	female: [0,1]; FRL: [0,1]
varcat	categorical	gender: [1,2]; achievement levels: [1,2,3,4]
varint	integer	days absent: [0,1,2...]; class size: [1,2,3...]
varcon	continuous	test score growth: ...-1.123...0...1.123...
varcod	codes	schools: [12345, 12346, 12347...]; courses: [101,102,201...]
varwts	weights	total students in school-level aggregate data, etc.

TABLE 7.3: String variable types

Name	Type	Example
varind	indicator	female: [Y,N]; FRL: [Yes, No,unknown]
varcat	categorical	days absent: ["1"=0-7days,"2"=8-15days,"3"=15+days]
varcod	codes	[012345, 012346, 012347...]

In practice, the classifications of variable types are more fluid. Discrete variables with many values, for instance, may be treated as continuous variables in some analysis. String and numeric variables may both contain positive and negative integers conveying other information about the data point, such as "not applicable" or flags for validation errors on missing values. Also, number values may be converted back and forth between string and numeric variable formats, so it is important to track that these get converted correctly.

In our variables shorthand that follows, when we need to distinguish string and numeric variables in the sample commands we'll add notation, such as `varnumcat` vs. `varstrcat`.

7.2.3.2 Observations

Observation levels can consist of combinations of the following: students, subjects, courses, semesters, years, schools, districts, states, subgroups of student demographics and/or special populations, and teachers. The following are examples of disaggregated and aggregated observation levels:

Disaggregated:

- **student-semester-year**
    - absences, suspensions, high school course grades
- **student-subject-year**
    - own test scores, peer mean scores
- **teacher-classroom-subject-year**
    - teacher value-added measure, class mean scores

Aggregated:

- **school-year-demographic**
    - enrollments, etc., per race/ethnicity and gender
- **school-year-grade-classification**
    - Algebra passing rates per grade by FRL, SWD, ELL

Now, we plug these shorthand variable types into our shortcut commands for creating quick, clean, informative tables and graphs.

7.2.4 Descriptive tools

Using the variables shorthand to create a set of command short-cuts for descriptives

Generally speaking, a frequency table consists of a single variable's values grouped by the number of occurrences, with counts and/or percentages and a running count and/or cumulative percentage. Cross-tabulations ("crosstabs") can be cross-frequency tables of the number of observations within each combination of the distinct variable values. These distinct values are the string and numeric categories, codes, and integers. These can include combinations of discrete string and/or numeric variables, as well as additional rows and columns for missing values and/or subtotals.

While a table of means generally provides sample mean values and standard deviations for a list of variables, often including minimum and maximum values and the n-value for the number of non-missing observations. These and other summary statistics, such as medians, percentile cutoffs or mean values, and interquartile ranges, etc., are meaningful for continuous, discrete, and (in some cases) indicator variables. In addition to reporting these statistics for the full sample, similar tabling commands and others can be used to report combinations of the summary statistics for these variables at the distinct value levels of additional "by" or "over" variables. Generally, these are categorical or discrete variables designated as the row and column and table variables, over which other discrete and/or continuous variables are summarized in cells and at row, column, and table levels.

Some data checks are not suited to tables of summary statistics. For instance, you are less likely to want to view test score values or other long lists of numeric data in tables. Instead, these are the types of variables you are more likely to view in distributional graphs and bar graphs. Use the graphs to visualize their means, cumulative sums, and other summary values, for the full samples and separately at distinct groupings of important categorical variables (see Figure 6.2 in the previous chapter for an example.) We begin with the tables, and then we provide shortcut commands for these histograms and bar graphs further below.

7.2.5 Descriptions: summary statistics

Overview of the summary commands

In Stata there are a number of different commands for describing data in table form. Please note that we are not focused on formatted tables here. There are separate subroutines for report-style formatted tables with all the good labeling and spacing options that you likely use for your production stage. But we're focusing here on the short command lines to keep littered throughout your data prep programs, and interactively in your data prep sessions, for frequent readable (and savable) descriptive output to keep tabs on your data transformations.

The `summarize` (or `sum`) command generates a simple table of basic summary statistics for each variable listed. `tabulate` or `tab` for short, can be a single one-way tabulations (or "tabs"), a two-way tab, a single command for a series of one-way tabs, and a single command for all combinations of a two-way tabs. It also allows for missings to be reported, variables to use value labels or not, and for values in rows, columns, and cells to be included and reported as frequencies and/or percentages. `tabstat` is another powerful command to use. It allows for a wide range of statistics, such as medians and percentiles, and formatting options for number of decimal places. It is ideal for reporting the same summary statistics for up to five similar variables. `table` is an ideal command for viewing combinations of summary statistics for a few different variables and for adding dimensions to view nxn tables (though three is the practical limit).

All of these commands can use the common additional features for further customizing what is tabulated or summarized. For instance, they can run the tables separately by the discrete values of an additional variable, They can filter the values to be summarized by including "if" statements, and they can accommodate weights. We also quickly cover the `codebook` and `compare` commands.

We list different specifications for each command, with its abbreviation and options both highlighted in bold, and with different variable types used as examples. We begin with the summary table commands.

Summary or sum

Only the numeric variables will report values—even the number of observations—but the command will run with the string variables included. The `codebook` command can be used for string values to get frequencies (to identify the number of missing values) and the type and range of text values, with the `compact` option for streamlining.

`sum` varcon1-varcon20, `sep(0)` (use any variable list, and use sep option to format)

Tabulate and tab

`tabulate` or `tab`, `tab1`,`tab2`, `tab sum()`, `tab1 sum()`

Where varind#, varcat#, and varcod# are numeric or string, and where varcod# and varint# do not have too many values (with the longest value set variable listed first):

```
tab varind1
// (gives frequencies, percentages, and cumulative percentages)


tab varcat1
// (can do any of the ind, cat, code, or int variables)


tab varind1, mis
// (add this option to includes cells for missing values)


tab1 varind1 varcat1 varind2 varcat2
// (generates each of the four tabs)


bysort varind1: tab varcat1
// (tabs varcat1 for each varind1 and then for all or total)
```

```
tab varcat1 varind1
// (crosstabs varcat1 in rows by varind1 in columns with totals)

tab varcod1 varcat1
// (can crosstab long value-set variable as rows)

tab2 varind1 varcat1 varind2 varcat2
// (generates each of the six crosstabs)
```

```
tab varcat1 varind1, row col cell nofreq nokey
/*
(replaces frequencies with individual and total percentages for any
 combination of row, col, and/or cell, while specifying nofreq makes
 the percentages table easier to read and nokey just skips the extra
 key output)
*/

tab varcat1 [aw=varwts1]
// (analytic weight option generates weighted freqs or pcts)

tab varcat1, sum(varcon1)
//(gives means of the continuous variable for each category)

tab1 varcat1, sum(varcon1)
//(can combine tab1 and tab, sum)
```

Note, this tab command is best to use for the only statistics that can be reported for string variables, which is the frequency of observations under each text value. Tab is set up to easily choose and view combinations of Ns and percentages with cumulative percentages for one variable, and cell, row, and column values for more than one. These next, more sophisticated tabulation commands also calculate frequencies, but they are primarily designed to generate a wider range of statistics for numeric variables.

Tabstat

With `tabstat`, a number of summary statistics can easily be selected to view in the same quick table for a subset of variables. Note the formatting option is good to use to control decimal places (i.e., 0 for summary integer values, and 2 or 4 for percentages, depending on the variable). Other formatting options let you alter the defaults for when statistics are listed along rows or columns. The statistics can be generated at each value of an added "by" variable. And while the subset of variables for which the statistics are generated must be numeric, the added variable they are broken out over can be either string or numeric. Different combinations of variable types in these different positions produce a range of quick, useful descriptives.

```
tabstat varcon1, stat(n mean sd min max q iqr)
/*
  (reports statistics like these in one long row for the
    one continuous variable)
*/


tabstat varcon1-varcon8, stat(n mean sd min max q iqr)
/*
  (reports each statistic in a row under each continuous
    variable column heading)
*/


tabstat varind1 varind2 varind3, stat(mean) format(%9.4f)
*/ (can use with binary indicators to report sample
    percentages, here to 2 decimal places)
*/


tabstat varcon1 varcon2 varcon3, by(varcat1) stat(mean)
*/ (gives the means of continuous variables by each value
    of a single categorical variable)
*/
```

```
tabstat varcon1 varcon2 varcon3, by(varstrcat1) stat(mean)
// (can do the same with a string formatted categorical variable)

tabstat varcon1 varcon2 varcon3, by(varcod1) stat(mean)
/* (also useful for quickly listing means or other stats
    for all schools or districts) */

tabstat varind1 varind2 varind3, by(varcod1) stat(mean)
/* (and for reporting percentages for all schools, etc.,
    from binary variables)*/
```

Table

The `table` command allows for multiple "by" string or numeric variables for statistics to be generated over. It also allows for different combinations of statistics to be generated for different subsets of numeric variables of interest. This way, you can quickly generate a 2x2 or 3x3 table with means generated for one of the numeric variables of interest, medians for another, and frequencies for a third, etc. The "c" in the table command is short for "contents" of the table, and adding the options row and col gets you the stats at those levels as well.

Technically, the limits are five content variables, three table dimensions, and seven additional, nested "by" variables. However, these barebones tables get a little hard to read with too many dimensions or too much content. (And if you go to three dimensions you'll want to put the longest value-set variable in the third position.)

```
table varstrind1 varstrind2 varcat1,
   c(n varcon1 mean varcon2 mean varcon3) row  col

/* (generates different content statistics by combinations
    of the 3 table dimension variables)*/
```

```
table varind1 varind2 varcat1, by(varcat1 varcat2)
  c(mean varcon1 mean varcon2)

/* (note: you can extend the dimensions with additional
    "by" or "over" variables)*/
```

Compare

There's just one last command we cover here under descriptors before moving to the depicter graphing short command lines. This is the `compare` command. It very simply compares the values in two variables. It reports the number of observations that are jointly defined, so you see each variable's missing values relative to the other. It counts the number of observations for which the values are equal, those where the value in the first variable listed is greater than the second, and where it's less than the second. All this is done for string variables as well as numeric (where, for instance, "Yes" is alphabetically greater than "No"). Then, for numeric variables, it gives the min, mean, and max values for the differences overall and separately for negative and positive values. This is a great way to quickly check on variables you thought or hoped would be similar.

```
compare var1source1 var1source2
/* (gives # jointly defined, and #, min, mean, max for var1source1 >
    and < var1source2)*/

compare var1constructed var1initial
/* (can be used to check variables you constructed to address
    something like missings)*/
```

7.2.6   Depictions: graphs of distributions and relationships

Overview of summary depictions

As mentioned, the two quickest visual data descriptions that you can easily incorporate into your data prep work are the variable distributions and bar graphs. These show you most of what you need to know to be checking on the range and concentration of values within each variable of interest, individually and across the value sets of additional numeric or string variables.

Histogram variable distributions

As a rule of thumb, histograms are preferable to tabulations when you are trying to get a quick look at the distribution of a continuous variable or a discrete variable with many values. You can also view the distributions for a variable broken out by the categories of another variable. And remember that you can add "if" statements of the variable of interest to zoom in closer on specific ranges of the variable, or you can use them to filter on other variables. The histogram is preferable to the continuous distribution graphs, such as the kernal-densities, for the purposes of checking your data, because they allow you to read values off the axis that correspond to the frequency Ns and percentages of the tabulation tools discussed above.

```
histogram varcon1,  density
// (density is the default, the total area sums to one)

histogram varcon1,  frequency
/* (heights of each bar or bin give number of observations
    and their sum equals total sample)
   (heights can also give the percent or fraction, and
    sum to 100 or 1)
  (either the bin number or width can also be specified,
    as well as a start value) */

histogram varcat1, discrete percent
/* (sets number of bins equal to number of discrete values,
    with heights giving percentages) */

histogram varcon1, by(varind1, col(1) total)
```

```
/* (lines up three histograms is a single row, one
      for each indicator value and one for total) */

histogram varcon1, normal
// (overlays a normal curve on top of the histogram)
```

Simple bar graphs

There are a number of very useful two-way graphs even at the descriptive prep stages. Scatter plots are useful for individual classes or schools or for aggregated data, but we're focusing on the kinds of graphs you can quickly read the summary statistics off of as well as view general shapes and ranges. The class size histogram and smoothed curve in 7.1 was more thoughtfully formatted than most of the simple descriptive data prep work you'll do in-house.

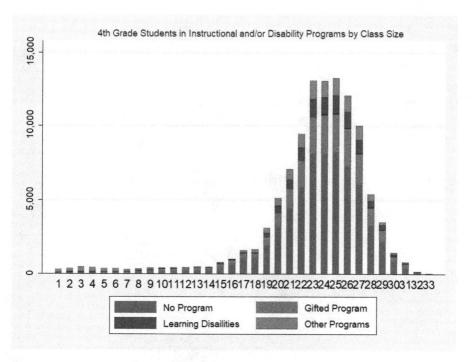

FIGURE 7.2: Simple stacked bar graph shows student programs throughout class sizes.

Figure 7.2, with a class size bar graph of students in instructional programs, is more representative of the quick and dirty formatting you can fold into your work habits. For these types of descriptive explorations, clearly labeling the categories and sample you're exploring is important, but aesthetics are not.

To make these bar graphs versatile and still readable, we are covering more formatting options below.

```
graph bar varcon1
/* (single bar with height equal to the mean
    of the continuous variable, since default is mean) */

graph bar varcon1 varint1
/* (two bars with heights equal to the mean of the continuous
    and the integer variable) */

graph bar varcont1, over(varcat1)
/* (a bar for each value of varcat1, with heights equal to
    the mean of varcon1) */

graph bar varcon1 varcon2, over(varcat1)
/* (two bars for each value of varcat1, with heights equal
    to means of varcon1 and varcon2) */

graph bar mean varcon1 median varcon1, over(varcat1)
/* (two bars for each value of varcat1, with heights equal to
    varcon1 mean and median) */

graph bar varcon1 varcon2, over(varcat1) percentage stack
/* (stacked bars of the means, here as percentages totaling 100,
    for each value of varcat1) */

graph bar varcont1, over(varcat1) over(varcat2)
/* (set of bars with varcont1 mean for each value of varcat1,
    nested in set of varcat2 values) */
graph bar varcont1,
```

```
over(varcod1, sort(1) label(labsize(vsmall) angle(vertical)))
/* (bars labelled over many values, such as school codes, and
   sorted in order of varcon1)*/
```

7.3   Conclusion

To steal from T. S. Elliot...

"Immature poets imitate; mature poets steal..."

Our hope in writing this guide—and this chapter in particular—is that you cut and paste our text into your work shamelessly! Nothing would make us happier than to know you're making your data more your own by making our expertise yours.

CHAPTER 8

Conclusion

Through this book, we set out to give folks starting in this field a leg up with understanding how administrative data gets used in education organizations. Our goal was to provide insight into the critical pieces of the craft that often go overlooked in academic or policy focused depictions of education data work.

Yes, it is important to get your standard errors right in a regression model in the end, but much more critical is all the work that happens before you ever type *reg* into your software.

We hope if you've made it this far, you have found value in the perspectives we've shared and in the recommendations we've made. There is so much potential for high quality and responsive data analysis to improve how education systems function, and we hope this book helps you and your agency along the path of using more and better analytics.

If you are pressed for time (and we know you are!) here's a recap of what we think are the most important takeaways from each chapter and how these pieces fit together into a broader whole.

8.1   Metadata

In Chapter 2, we began where all analysis should begin - with the metadata. Metadata is how we know what our data mean and how we can evaluate their provenance. Our main points on this were:

1. Excellent metadata and business rule documentation are like the Holy Grail. Extraordinary, perhaps mythical, and imbued with amazing power to enable those who hold them to do incredible things.
2. If your institution doesn't have a data dictionary, you should try to build one, but you shouldn't do this alone. You should bring together the other data folks in your organization to undertake this quest together (preferably at a Round Table[1]). Your collective knowledge will be important in doing this work well.
3. Your IT colleagues can help you with this effort and you should include them. They may have important insight to contribute.
4. This quest is never really over (read: done). It's a living, ongoing effort, much like any epic adventure[2].

8.2   Analyst's Guide to IT

After covering metadata, in Chapter 3 we moved on to talk about how analysts and IT departments can work together to improve both the metadata and the operating efficiency of analysts in Chapter 3. We found that a lot of our on-the-job learning was about how to work well with IT departments and learn their ways. Our main thoughts we hope you gleaned from this chapter were:

1. Working with IT staff and your agency's IT infrastructure is critical to success in your job.
2. IT colleagues have a lot of expertise in building and supporting long-term data applications - these techniques can help you automate and build sustainable work.

---

[1] https://en.wikipedia.org/wiki/Knights_of_the_Round_Table

[2] https://en.wikipedia.org/wiki/Hero%27s_journey

3. IT has its own terms of art that can be off-putting at first, but if you can learn them and use them, you'll be able to work even better with your colleagues.

4. If you build a strong, durable relationship with IT, you can partner to do powerful things for your organization. You can teach one another a lot and grow together into a formidable team that solves problems and serves your institution better together than you ever could separately.

8.3 Data Requests

In Chapter 4, we switched gears and started talking about practical tasks as a way of illustrating how metadata and IT operations play out in the day to day work of the agency. Data requests provide an excellent case study for how agencies use data because every agency receives data and analysis requests. Those requests always touch on issues of metadata, data governance, and IT operations. Our main takeaways on data requests were:

1. Data requests are a great opportunity to pressure test and build out your data governance solutions. Providing data outside of your organization is exactly the kind of action that data governance processes exist to manage.

2. Data requests can be burdensome, but the burden can also be managed with organization, prioritization, automation, and documentation.

3. Data requests should never be a one-way street — think about strategic applications of data requests where you can get something of value back from the request — a report, an analysis, documentation of changes to how an element can be used. The possibilities are there. Take some time to think about what you want to get back

from the partners you're providing the information to.

4. Deepening existing data request and data sharing agreements instead of taking on additional requests (also known as "learning to say 'no' ") can help turn data requests from an organizational chore into an organizational asset. Value-added relationships can be built this way.

8.4   Bureaucracy and Politics

After talking about how data requests fit into an organization, we turned our attention to navigating the organization itself in Chapter 5, Bureaucracy.

We all entered our roles with big ideas about how to change technical or operational things and make them better, but we quickly learned there was a whole set of skills about how to approach change in an education agency in general that we needed to learn first. In this chapter we cover some of the main concepts that help in understanding why an organization operates the way it does, and what we as analysts can do within that organization.

1. Building organizational change by leveraging data requires skills other than technical data analysis and management skills — you need organizational thinking.
2. Organizations don't change rapidly because the larger they are, the more people need to participate in the decision. At the same time, organizations also prioritize more immediate benefits over long-term benefits, since the members of the organization may not be long-game oriented.
3. Information is the currency inside of an organization — information helps the organization do everything. Information is traded internally and the organization trades

information externally for things like bigger budgets, new programs, and other things. Analysts are in a unique position because of their ability to produce and examine information for the organization.

4. As an analyst, you can use the timeliness, accuracy, and clarity of the information you produce to help build organizational change.

8.5   The Power of Descriptives

Finally, in Chapters 6 and 7 we talk about the power of descriptive analyses in an agency. While an awful lot of the focus in our training tends to be on inferential methods, much of the demand from within our organizations is for high quality descriptive work. And, as a bonus, high quality descriptive work will always make inferential work better. So, ultimately we think it's important to speak up on behalf of descriptive work and highlight how critical it is to building a successful data culture in an education agency.

1. Analysing patterns in administrative data with descriptive tools to fully understand the data themselves is some of the most important–but often overlooked–work you'll need to carry out.
2. Descriptive analysis is essential to better understand all the data that could be used in-house or with external researchers to make inferences for policy or practice.
3. Three main stages to implement descriptive analytic practices are: while working with the raw data files, when prepping raw data to generate extracts for research purposes, and when preparing an analytic dataset for research.
4. Three rules for carrying out descriptive analytics well: explore the data with descriptives before conducting any analysis, run the descriptives yourself (i.e., in-house), doc-

ument and share what you learn–especially regarding before/after and rationale of any analytic dataset refinement decisions.

The second of these two chapters takes the conversation a bit further. We couldn't put this book together and skip talking a little bit about tools or give some concrete examples. We hope future volumes (and we're looking squarely at you as a potential contributor right now) provide some more detailed guides on how to approach education data challenges, including those presented by using inferential statistics, but for now, this is where we start.

The descriptive analysis tools that we return to time and time again - the greatest hits - deserve attention and care. They can do a lot, including tell you what you can't do with the data, and we have found these tools and techniques to be as powerful, if not more, in policy discussions than just about anything else around:

1. Applied descriptive methods are described as two types: descriptions of data through summary statistics including cross-tabulations, and depictions of data through graphs including histograms.
2. Three main components of the data that need further exploration and refinement before and throughout the data prep stages are: variable formats and structures, value content meanings and missings, and observation subsets, frequencies, and duplicates.
3. Stata command line syntax provided is organized around these components and descriptive types, with tips on useful option settings and quick, clear output that's ideal for documenting what you find.

Ultimately, these two chapters are only a beginning. We've selected the issues that we think matter most and where we think there is the least existing practical guidance on how to proceed. We hope it proves helpful to you and your teams in the critical work you are doing.

Finally, we hope you've read this text as the call to action we wrote it to be. We want to invite you to join us in this work. We plan to keep the conversation going and build out a more complete set of resources.

We invite you to contribute to future volumes, highlighting the efforts from the trenches and the lessons you've learned so we can all do good science, together.

This is about doing the work right - the small things done well consistently. It's about the little details that are hugely consequential. We hope that this text has helped make doing that important work well even a little bit easier.